MW01241713

DREAMS REMEMBERED

A Memoir

by

Jackie L. Caldwell

as told to Vicki Bomke Thomson

iUniverse, Inc.
New York Bloomington

Dreams Remembered
A Memior

iUniverse books may be ordered through booksellers or by contacting:

iUniverse
1663 Liberty Drive
Bloomington, IN 47403
www.iuniverse.com
1-800-Authors (1-800-288-4677)

ISBN: 978-1-4401-0141-0 (sc)
ISBN: 978-1-4401-2745-8 (dj)
ISBN: 978-1-4401-0143-4 (ebk)

Printed in the United States of America

iUniverse Rev. 6/30/2009

To Cynthia,
who always brought out the best in me.

"Jackie, one day I know you will enjoy some kind of success. The only thing I ask of you today is that when you get up and look in the mirror, don't you see that silver. You see Jackie. If you see silver, you're going to let money control your life. I never want you to be in a situation where you look down at people with less."

Catherine Britton
1957

FOREWORD

Throughout the forty-six years we were married, my wife encouraged me to write an autobiography. Some adventures, she often said, were too fantastic not to share. Several weeks after Cynthia's passing, I decided to make her suggestion a reality. The process was not always easy; however, retracing and recording the episodes that shaped my life proved to be both therapeutic and enlightening. I now better appreciate my journey—the way one human being impacts another, the ripple effect a single decision can wield, and, ultimately, an understanding that even the smallest defeat or triumph serves a purpose.

Of course, Cynthia was right. *Dreams Remembered* includes a generous helping of the unusual and incredible. It is my hope and prayer that others will benefit from reading its contents long after I am gone.

Jackie L. Caldwell

1.

Even though I had never considered myself a great dancer, moving to the music came naturally that balmy May evening in 2006. Dressed in turquoise and white, my wife looked incredibly stunning, and I, as usual, was smitten. That night, Cynthia felt small, frail, and wonderfully familiar in my arms at the Hotel Peabody ballroom in downtown Memphis. For a few sweet moments, we almost forgot her illness. As the final notes of "Save the Last Dance for Me" concluded my high school reunion, I felt blessed beyond words.

Returning to my roots put things in perspective for me. I had not always been so fortunate in life, but it felt good to slow down and gather my memories. Individual episodes came to mind, like pieces of a challenging puzzle—each so different, yet every one dependent on the other to make a whole. My jigsaw of fate began more than six decades ago, scarcely thirteen miles away.

Mama claimed that I had a rough start in life. More than once she told me that we were the only two in the room when I entered this world on April 11, 1940. My earliest recollection, however, begins in the summer of 1943, during a period when the United States was actively engaged in World War II.

In my rural hometown of Parkin, Arkansas, as in countless venues across the United States, government-issued stamps were required for everyday necessities such as sugar, shoes, and tires. As a young child, I didn't understand why many things once taken for granted were now scarce. In fact, I didn't know the difference. Because my parents were sharecroppers—the poorest of the poor—every cent earned or saved was precious.

The St. Francis River, only a stone's throw from our wood-frame, shotgun-style house, was best known for its alligator garfish; however, my family was more interested in the treasure trove of mussels that carpeted its muddy floor. The real worth of this homely crustacean was not found in its gritty meat, but in its shell. Each such covering was uniquely beautiful and in big demand for garment buttons. In fact, one shell could be turned into several such gems at a plant in nearby Memphis, Tennessee. To supplement our family's meager income, my father often dove for mussels from a fourteen-foot wooden plank he had installed at the river's edge. It was to that very platform that I found myself precariously heading one August afternoon.

"Hurry up, Jackie," chirped my big sister. At the age of five, Bobbie was only two years my senior, but she both mothered and protected me. Bobbie was my idol, and I trusted her completely.

"Yeah, come on," my seven-year-old brother added. "You're slowing us down." As usual, Jimmy wanted to be in charge. Dark haired and handsome, he was not much taller than me. He spoke with the voice of authority, but ours was not a friendly relationship. From the beginning, I had no doubt that Jimmy wished that I had not been born. In our family, he was the first child, the first boy, and the first grandchild. My arrival had upset his apple cart. Even so, I was not intimidated by his jealousy.

Although I knew this was a journey my parents strictly forbade, it seemed downright reasonable in the company of my older siblings. My small, bare feet scurried to make contact with the rough wood of Daddy's makeshift diving board. More excited than hesitant, I inched toward the edge and gazed into the murky depths below. The racing water, turned smoky teal by the setting sun, was mesmerizing.

Whack! I both heard and felt a hard blow between my shoulder blades. The powerful jolt propelled my tiny body into a liquid abyss more dense and scary than my young imagination could comprehend. Feeling unbelievably helpless, I struggled to reach the surface. The harder I fought to stay above water, the more of the St. Francis River I swallowed.

"Help!" I wailed as the water muffled my plea. "Help! Hel … He …"

The rushing water, which eventually flowed into the vast White River, naturally gained momentum as it came around the bend. The surging current had no trouble carrying my body downstream at a dizzying pace. Like a cork bobber playing tag with a hungry fish, I continued to sink, only to resurface, choking and gasping for a few precious gulps of air.

Surely guardian angels exist on earth, because God sent one to my rescue that day. I looked up to see the slender form of my sister, running along the riverbank. "Hold on!" she screamed over the roaring water.

Somehow, Bobbie—also clueless about swimming—mustered the courage to jump in and paddle in my direction. Instinctively, she grabbed my short pants, again and again. Knowing that Bobbie had taken charge, I felt my tense body relax. Without warning, my world went black, and I turned blue.

When I awoke in the tall weeds of the shore, the sky was considerably darker, and Bobbie was nestled next to me in an exhausted heap. Her brown eyes blinked, then widened, as she untwisted a single pink barrette from her dark, matted hair. For a moment, we gazed at each other with mutual relief. Then reality kicked in.

"We gotta get back quick before Mama and Daddy find out," she squealed, frantically shaking me and springing to her feet. "Hurry, Jackie!"

Coughing, I followed my sister's lead. We raced toward home, gingerly dodging the sharp shells and underbrush. Muddy from head to toe, Bobbie and I were unable to conceal our little secret. We both knew there would be a price to pay for our awful adventure. Sure enough, my father was impatiently waiting in the distance, brandishing the belt he had extracted from his khaki pants.

Standing five feet ten inches tall, Verldon Gordon Caldwell was not a large man; however, to us kids, he was formidable. Discipline was a part of his personality. Although Daddy never missed an opportunity to teach us right from wrong, he didn't always practice what he preached. I was just learning that "do as I say" rarely meant "do as I do." Bobbie and I never protested or questioned our punishment, particularly on this sticky summer evening.

While we dutifully accepted a round of swift swats, Jimmy, the pusher, hid under the porch. My brother, who had made no effort to save me, was the guiltiest of all, and I think the episode scared him the most. Because our house was elevated on cinder blocks, his presence was obvious.

Daddy squatted down to peer at Jimmy, who crouched in the shadows. My brother looked as frightened as a hound dog caught sucking eggs from the henhouse.

"Look, you can spend the whole night there if you like, but it's not going to change anything," Daddy promised. My father removed his signature fedora hat and rolled up the sleeves of his white work shirt to lay flat on the ground, putting him almost eye to eye with the culprit. "You might as well come out and take your punishment."

The threats persisted until dusk: Jimmy reluctantly surrendered to Daddy's coaxing, and Bobbie and I watched with glee as my father kept his word. I can still hear him asking, "Do you know why you're gettin' a whuppin'? Son, do you know why you're gettin' a whuppin'?"

2.

I watched Mama and Daddy pick cotton dozens of times, but one morning, probably around October of 1944, takes center stage. A slight chill hung in the air as dawn prepared to break. Slowly the sun floated to the horizon and found a spot overhead to rest. In the bright light, my parents' tanned faces looked weary beyond their twenty-something years. Daddy, whose side of the family turned gray early, looked even older than Mama.

Even at four years of age, I was bright enough to sense that there had to be a better way to make a living. I often heard Mama tell Daddy that they were supposed to earn half of the crop cost. For whatever reason, the arrangement never happened quite that way. Early in life, I respected my mother as both the breadwinner and the backbone of our family. A hard worker with a good head for business, she definitely set the pace. Mama also made sure that we were clean and had clean clothes to wear. She always provided enough love—just not enough money—to go around.

Sharecropping was a family affair. With Bobbie and Jimmy now old enough to attend grade school, I inherited the responsibility of babysitting my younger siblings, Billy Ray, about three years old, and Patsy, barely a year, while our parents toiled. Young as we were, we knew better than to complain about the endless heat and boredom.

As Mama and Daddy worked the fields, their harvest was deposited in a special on-site enclosure known as the cotton pen. When at capacity, the small structure was capable of storing about fifteen hundred pounds of raw cotton. More importantly, the patch of dirt outlined by a battered wood frame doubled as a playhouse for us kids. We took great delight in the realm of our imaginary world.

In reality, our family lived in pioneer conditions, without electricity or gas, so all fires for cooking and heating started with matches. I honestly don't remember where the matches came from that I so tightly cupped in my hands that day.

"Watch this," I announced, knowing my little brother, Billy Ray, was a willing audience.

"Hey, whatcha doin'?" he asked. His blue eyes widened. He looked up to me, and I enjoyed being his hero. With his stocky frame, sandy hair, and fair complexion, people often commented on how much we looked alike.

"You'll see," I announced, confident that I could brush the stick against the side of the cotton pen to produce fire. I thought back to how Daddy always did it. The process was the closest thing I knew to magic. Of course, I had no plan of what to do if my actions were successful.

As if on cue, the match hissed and lit on the first try. Fascinated, I observed as the short flame lifted its head, fueled by the very breeze that was so gentle a few seconds earlier. My awe quickly turned to terror as a gust of wind transported the red-hot match into the full cotton pen that surrounded us. In an instant, a thick layer of smoke concealed my siblings, and it was difficult to see where the blaze started or stopped. To make matters worse, the acrid fumes penetrated my throat and nostrils. I choked on my own breath.

The three of us were in deep trouble. Patsy had disappeared, but I had no trouble finding Billy Ray. He was squealing at the top of his lungs and clinging tightly to my leg. I, too, was scared. Never questioning my own strength, I stumbled and maneuvered the two of us across the sod floor and away from the leaping flames. We had almost reached safety when I looked up to see my frantic parents running toward us. Mama was clutching the hand of a coughing and crying Patsy, whose delicate skin and light hair were covered in sweat. She had apparently fallen, and her cheeks were scratched and smeared with grime. To my relief, Daddy pried Billy Ray—still spellbound by the fiery spectacle—away from me. His flushed face was the color of ripe beets.

A fear unlike any other consumed me. I darted in the opposite direction, running far into the woods until I could run no more. Scarce as money was, I knew that burning up the month's harvest would only make life harder.

It took every bit of those fifteen hundred pounds of unginned cotton to equal five hundred pounds, or one bale, of ginned cotton. In those days, my parents worked a month to produce the bale I had unintentionally destroyed. A single bale was worth approximately three hundred dollars, and, as sharecroppers, my parents expected to receive 50 percent of the profits. No doubt Mama and Daddy were glad that Billy Ray, Patsy, and I had survived the fire, but losing that income certainly made our lot in life just that much more difficult to overcome. Even so, I don't recall my parents ever discussing the incident again.

3.

Times may have been financially trying, but our surroundings were rich with simple pleasures. In Cross County, a picnic went hand in hand with good weather. When spring came, it was a chance to breathe fresh air after being cooped up all winter. By summer, a picnic provided a welcome break in the routine. Later in the year, the outing was a rite of passage, a final farewell to warm weather. For sure, every bite of food tasted better at a picnic.

Sometimes my cousin Pat joined the party while Mama and her sister-in-law, my Aunt Oley, visited. Our mothers were good friends, and at first glance, polar opposites. Beautiful inside and out, Aunt Oley was a thin, frail woman with long, dark hair and olive-toned skin. Rain or shine, she was the picture of femininity in her long, floral-print dresses. My mother, Opal Shaw Caldwell, was pretty in her own way, with full, dark brown hair and light skin. She had boundless stamina, and quite literally wore the pants in our family. In fact, she wore my dad's khakis most of the time. At five feet five inches tall, with a medium build, Mama wasn't particularly large, but she was strong and sturdy. My mother was from a hard-working family and had an overabundance of energy. She simply could not be outworked.

While our moms cooked and chattered, Billy Ray, Pat, Patsy, and I took great care in mixing dirt with rainwater and then cutting the slimy dough with a can to produce mud pies. When we were satisfied, our shiny, uneven creations were lined up and ready to bake in the sunshine.

"Wash up," Mama always called. "Your picnic is almost ready." She never had to ask twice. After a morning of playing outside, we were ready to eat a lunch of Rex strawberry jam and biscuits. Even my dog, Poochie, the eighty-pound, short-haired yellow canine who adopted me, got friskier at the suggestion. It was as though he hung on our every word.

"Yum," Billy Ray said, smacking his lips.

"Thanks, Aunt Opal," said Pat. "Just what I'm hungry for!" Quiet and slim, my cousin was three years my junior. It was good to see her eat, although she never seemed to gain weight.

With Christmas two and one-half months away, we were already compiling our wish lists. While we ate, the four of us pored over the Sears & Roebuck catalog. I am certain that none of our parents had an account, but just the same, every household received a catalog. In fact, my grandfather once ordered a black automobile, similar to a Ford Model A, from the retail giant. In my childhood, the book's slick, multicolored pages provided hours of entertainment—more fantasy than reality—as we idly wished for what we didn't have and lacked the means to purchase.

"Hey, look at that!" cooed Billy Ray, pointing to a photo of a shiny red tricycle. Having never seen such a vehicle, we were instantly drawn to its wordy description, sporting inches of text that none of us could read.

"Think Santa can bring that?" I wondered out loud. "I hope he does!"

Pat and I continued to scan the kaleidoscope of pages and soak in the rainbow of clothing worn by smiling children about our ages. We longingly gazed over the endless variety of denim fashions, noticeably free of telltale patches and any hint of hand-me-down status. Somehow we all knew that the possibility of procuring any such item from Santa—or, for that matter, Sears & Roebuck—existed only in our heads.

I don't remember what my cousin, sisters, and older brother received, but that Christmas Santa brought a toy pistol for Billy Ray and a new pair of coveralls for me. Santa also delivered a little bit of fruit—mostly apples and oranges—and a few nuts.

4.

In today's world, responsible parents would not think of leaving four children under the age of seven years at home alone until the wee hours of the morning. As little kids, we were left alone—a lot. I guess Mama and Daddy must have felt the need to escape their everyday stress and enjoy a good time. Those were some of the rare times when we heard our parents laugh, so we never really minded if their dates took them away for a few hours. Sometimes it was way past midnight when they returned. If we were lucky, my dad had a surprise for us. When watermelons were in season, he'd arrive home with a ripe one for us to cool off in a tub. Savoring the juicy red fruit is one of the happiest memories of my childhood. To this day, I still love a good watermelon.

With each birthday came new responsibilities, and 1945 was no different. That year I acquired a host of jobs, one of which was riding the extra horse to deliver water to Daddy in the fields. I also was able to hunt for food. For my fifth birthday, Pa Shaw, my maternal grandfather, gave me a twenty-two caliber rifle and taught me the basics of shooting by using a Prince Albert tobacco can for target practice.

Meat was a rarity, and a kill of rabbits, birds, or squirrels was much appreciated, especially by Mama. With Poochie by my side, I was never afraid to go anywhere. At a time in life when a young boy should have a dog, Poochie was the ideal pal. The two of us savored many hunting excursions in the Arkansas woods. If we were lucky, we'd also find wild possum grapes, hog apples, or dewberries along the ditch's bank. More than once, an expedition would yield fresh honey from a hollow oak tree.

Chopping wood for home heating and cooking became another of my duties. At first, I was pretty aggressive and actually believed that I could tackle the task as well as those much older. However, life has a way of evening things out. One afternoon, just as I was feeling smug about my proficiency, I got the scare of my young life. Engrossed in my task, I didn't hear or see my cousin Pat walk up behind me as I was chopping a fallen oak tree. Startled by her presence, I neglected to cover my axe, which made contact with her face, as I suddenly turned around. Blood spurted everywhere. When my poor cousin yelped in pain, my first thought was that I had killed her. Fortunately, my mother's clothesline broke the momentum of my swing, and so Pat's wound was not life threatening. More than sixty years later, she still bears a slight scar from a split lip.

In our part of the country, farms still operated much the same as they had in the previous century, and progress moved at a snail's pace. After working all week, on Saturday we sometimes traveled into "town"—a settlement four miles away known as Gesick—to buy groceries. Our shopping list was dictated by available cash as well as storability. Refrigeration was a luxury, and it came quite literally in the form of an icebox. The ice man delivered ice only if the customer paid in advance and left a sign ordering the number of pounds needed. Not surprisingly, we hardly ever had anything cold to drink.

Sundays were reserved for faith, relatives, and feasting. Our family lived three miles from my maternal grandparents' house, and it was at least another four miles to church. My eager legs carried me to both.

After services, my grandmother always prepared a delicious dinner. Indeed, it was a spread I looked forward to sampling all week. To understand why I anticipated this meal more than those at our house, it's necessary to first know my family's day-to-day dining habits. Our meals consisted of biscuits—sometimes with molasses and butter—for breakfast, beans and potatoes for lunch, and cornbread for supper. In spring, Mama cooked wilted salad, a combination of leaf lettuce, radishes, and green onions, topped by hot bacon grease. I could never get enough of that dish and still love it.

By contrast, a meal at my grandmother's table was always special. Week after week, the menu boasted produce—new potatoes, peas, corn on the cob, tomatoes, and butter beans—grown on their farm. Occasionally we had chicken, but a sumptuous variety of fresh vegetables was definitely the highlight.

These weekly gatherings also offered an opportunity to visit with three of my aunts who still lived with my grandparents. There was only a difference of seven years between me and my youngest aunt, so I probably grew up closer to my aunts than my cousins.

Some of my dearest memories involve my grandfather, a self-proclaimed redneck from Mississippi. To fully appreciate Pa Shaw, it's interesting to note that when he met my grandmother he was a widower with eight children. Upon his arrival in Arkansas, my grandfather purchased two hundred acres and eventually added more land. After he remarried, the acreage was manually cleared by Pa Shaw and his second family, a brood that grew to include eight more children.

The legendary Paul Bunyon had nothing on Pa Shaw. My grandfather was a small, wiry, and energetic man, no more than five feet six inches tall, but his hands were as big as a gorilla's. Pa Shaw was as strong as an ox with an appetite to match. He could eat as much as ten working-men, but he never got fat. Folks marveled at his ability to jump in and out of a fifty-gallon flour barrel in his bare feet.

Pa Shaw loved to fish almost as much as he loved to dip snuff and drink. It was no secret that when he drank, nobody worked. It was an equally well-known fact that when he fished, everybody fished. Another advantage of growing older was that I was allowed to go fishing with him. I relished those times at the lake, because a good catch of brim, crappie, or catfish guaranteed a family fish fry. Everything we fried was cooked in pork lard. Today it's said that too much fat will kill you, but, if that were true, I would have died long ago.

Once, when our winter food supply was running low, Pa Shaw and I took off with a fish seine, in hopes of snaring dinner. To my dismay, our efforts only yielded grinnel, a fish that tasted as bad as it was prehistorically ugly. At the very least, we had something to eat. We didn't starve.

Everywhere he went, Pa Shaw rode a horse as fine as money could buy, until he passed away in his sleep at the age of eighty-nine. Folks said that the day before his death, he helped a friend to harvest cotton.

Prepared for the inevitable, Pa Shaw had already made arrangements with the funeral home to be buried next to his first wife in Mississippi. Unlike her brothers and sisters, Mama respected his preference. There were hard feelings, but she had no qualms about carrying out his last wishes.

5.

The winter before I turned six years old was particularly cold. At night, the wind howled with a vengeance so strong that our four walls vibrated in protest. During the day when Jimmy and Bobbie were in school, Billy Ray and I huddled in the kitchen—the warmest room in the house—and amused ourselves by rolling a small can of Hunt's tomato sauce across the wood floor. My playmate giggled in anticipation as our improvised toy flipped over and over, then laughed excitedly when I spun it back to him. At four years of age, Billy Ray was good company, and we were as close as two peas in a pod when the water wasn't boiling.

Several mornings later, Billy Ray didn't want to play. In fact, he was unusually quiet, a sure indicator that something was seriously wrong. Within hours, my buddy was covered with red spots. Mama reached for his forehead and confirmed that he had a fever.

"Snooks," she told Daddy that night, "I think Billy Ray has the measles."

I saw my parents exchange glances, knowing that there was no money to pay a doctor. It wouldn't have mattered. Even if funds were available, there wasn't a doctor anywhere close to where we lived. Because Billy Ray had not started school, he also hadn't been vaccinated. Besides, Mama and Daddy agreed that shots were never a guarantee against illness.

At that time, Billy Ray and I shared a bed, so I felt and heard him toss and turn all night. In his fitful slumber, he moaned, "I wanna drink. Water, water . . ." every few minutes. I could tell by his soft, lonely cry that he felt miserable. It must have been about midnight that Mama brought a glass of water to my ailing brother.

"He's burning up," she whispered to my dad, just before I dozed off to sleep.

By morning, all was quiet when Mama came in to wake us. I wasn't sure where night left off and daylight started, but Billy Ray was no longer crying.

"How's Billy Ray?" I asked, turning over.

"I imagine he's catching up on his sleep," she said. "He's probably worn out from fighting that fever all night." I felt the mattress move as she tried to stir him.

"Oh, no! God, no!" Mama wailed. A scream unlike any other pierced the silence. That was the first time I ever saw my mother cry.

That week, our tiny house simmered in sadness as concerned friends and relatives came and went. Weary with grief, Mama wasn't the only one to cry, but her cry was the one that pained me the most. Times were hard enough without having to bury a child. I felt so small and helpless. Most of all, I wanted to turn back the clock and make Billy Ray well again.

"He needs a suit to be buried in," I overheard Mama tell Daddy.

"I'll have to borrow the money," he said. "Think ten dollars is enough?"

Although I had heard about death, now I really understood it. Even dressing Billy Ray in a new outfit would not bring him back.

At the cemetery, I could barely comprehend the minister's words. Trying to stand tall against the icy wind presented a challenge that was only compounded by well-meaning aunts, uncles, and cousins, who squeezed together to stay warm. Toward the end of the service, Mama grabbed my hand and led me to the open casket. I had not seen my brother up close until then and wasn't sure what to expect. Billy Ray looked so still and strange. His blond hair was tousled as usual, but his eyes had a faraway look.

"He's in heaven now," Mama said. With remarkable composure, she leaned down and gently closed his eyes.

Aunt Francis, Mama's younger and taller sister, stood next to me. I felt her hands, rough from working in the fields, insert two pennies in my clenched fist. She signaled for me to place the coins on top of Billy Ray's eyelids. I did as she requested and looked at my brother for one last time before the casket was closed.

As we walked away from Billy Ray's final resting place, I noticed that the grounds were sprinkled with light grey markers. Each appeared to have writing on it. Unlike the other graves, Billy Ray's had no marker.

6.

Billy Ray's passing left a huge void in my life. He had been my best friend, my playmate, and my companion. In truth, I could hardly remember when he wasn't around.

To make matters worse, a terrible accident happened when Mama was doing laundry several months later. While Poochie was snoozing beneath the wash table, my mother accidentally overturned an open bottle of lye. The corrosive liquid splashed on Poochie's back and burned straight through him. It was a quick death. I very much missed his company—from those adoring black eyes to his wagging tail—all the time. Now both of my buddies were gone.

Although Mama tried her best to cheer me up, she couldn't fill the emptiness I felt. After all, she had other kids, a husband, and a job to keep her busy. Naturally, Mama herself was still numb from Billy Ray's death. I desperately longed for the camaraderie of friends, and I found myself looking forward to starting school in the fall.

"Just think, Jackie," my mother said one night as she was preparing dinner. "Three days from now, you'll be in school." She patted my head and flashed a big smile. I couldn't decide which of us was more excited.

At the ripe, old age of six, I was ready to join my brother and sister in the pursuit of learning. Even though classes commenced the day after Labor Day, sharecroppers' kids did not actually attend classes for the first six weeks, because every set of hands, no matter how small, was needed to harvest the crops. I was cautiously optimistic about entering this new phase of my life. At last, it was my turn.

The evening before my first day of school, an injury threatened to ruin my plans. Tractors were new equipment for farming, and, although we still used mules, my dad had a tractor parked in the front of the house. In the shadows, I spotted what I thought was the eerie form of a human. Perched on the edge of our porch, I lost my balance and landed on top of a glass jar full of nuts and bolts. The jagged fragments punctured my foot, producing a cut deep enough to sever the nerves.

"Mama!" I screamed, as blood gushed everywhere. "Mama!"

The cut was secondary to the scariness of the figure, which I later learned was only the tractor's distorted silhouette in the moonlight. Unfortunately, the timing for an accident could not have been worse. The only medicine we had was kerosene, also known as coal oil, which was applied directly to the wound. My quick-thinking mother tore a bed sheet and wrapped my foot to stop the bleeding. The coal oil stung like the dickens, but I was determined not to miss my first day of first grade.

Even a throbbing foot could not dampen my spirits the next morning when I joined a class of about twenty students. Feeling like a big kid, I caught the school bus about 7:15 and was graciously greeted by my teacher, Miss Cox, on arrival. I was instantly enamored by this heavy-set, curly-haired brunette, who was no more than thirty years old.

"Welcome, honey!" she said, cheerfully. Her greeting was music to my ears.

Maybe it was the thrill of meeting my teacher or just being in a new and interesting place, but that morning I felt especially fortunate to have fifteen cents in my pocket. In fact, I was so excited that I spent a dime on a packaged ice cream bar and didn't have enough change left over for lunch. In a rare show of kindness, Jimmy gave me a little change to buy something in the cafeteria.

Although my routine changed because of school, there was never a break from chores. Before the sun rose, regardless of the weather, I pumped three tubs of water. This task was particularly important on Wednesday, when my mother washed clothes. With no machine to help her, the job took the entire day to complete. It was important to stay on schedule, because Thursday was her day to iron.

Our house had no electricity, so at night I studied by a kerosene lamp. It was a comfort that about a century before, Abraham Lincoln had done the same. There may have been many advances in the world since the youthful days of our sixteenth president, but in northeastern Arkansas, we still lived much the same way.

Within weeks, I became the best reader in the class. To this day, I can still remember that the first book I ever read was *Alice and Jerry* and how proud I was when Miss Cox sent me to the head table. I was also good in spelling, although penmanship wasn't my forte.

By the following year, I was an old hand at catching the school bus. My second-grade teacher was a fashion plate, and I thought she was quite beautiful. A slim woman in her twenties, Miss Jones kept her short brown hair coifed in the latest style and always dressed professionally in a skirt, blouse, and jacket. I had never known a woman who wore stockings all the time. To her credit, Miss Jones took her job seriously and saw to it that we mastered the three Rs: reading, 'riting, and 'rithmetic.

A full lunch in the cafeteria cost about fifteen or twenty cents, so most kids brought their lunches from home in three-pound lard cans. On most days, Mama packed me a biscuit with some molasses. It was a special treat when she included a little piece of side meat, usually salty pork that had been boiled before it was fried.

Our school day had two fifteen-minute recesses at mid-morning and early afternoon, but neither seemed long enough. Sometimes we played baseball and football; however, my favorite games involved marbles. Like all boys, I carried five or six marbles to school, including the largest marble, which was known as the toy. In addition to shooting marbles, we honed our skills in a game called drop bucket. The object of the game was to drop a marble from your waist through a hole drilled into a small can. If your marble went into the hole, you got to keep it. If you missed the hole, your opponent won the marble. I had an eagle's eye for the game and almost always hit the hole. In time, the other kids refused to let me play.

7.

As a youngster in the backwoods of Arkansas, I developed a close and personal relationship with nature. The Tyronza River, in particular, captured my imagination. In the grand court of creation, this natural phenomenon offers fitting testimony that Mother Nature wields a sense of humor. Rimmed by sandy, white shores with a sandbar midway between its banks, the Tyronza still resembles a beach more than a river. Tucked inside a thick canopy of pines, its clear waters empty into the St. Francis River to create a popular and magical swimming spot. For a curious kid, time exploring the Tyronza was pure joy. In fact, I never thought twice about walking the ten miles from Parkin to inspect its latest activity.

One crisp Sunday morning, two buddies and I agreed that the journey was worth the effort. We were awed by the aftermath of a powerful storm that had blown through the night before, forcing the river to run fast—some hundred miles per hour—while randomly scattering jagged hunks of driftwood in its path.

As Charles Westmoreland, Herbert Todd (known as Todd), and I traipsed closer, our hearts pounded with anticipation. It didn't take long before our third-grade egos took over. The predictable dares began.

"Bet you can't throw farther than me," said Charles. He smoothed his dark, curly hair with one hand and held a grey rock in the other. Charles was taller than Todd and me. We tried not to wince when he effortlessly hurled the rock at least a hundred feet.

"Bet I can," I boasted, without thinking twice.

"Me, too," echoed Todd. His roots were in hunting and fishing, but he was an athlete to the core.

We took turns trying to beat Charles, but our efforts failed. Both of our rocks sailed through the air, only to fall short of their targets. Because we were also teammates in baseball, more than a throwing contest was at stake.

"Never mind," Charles said. "Bet this one skips longer than both of yours." His hand opened to reveal a clay-colored pebble as smooth as any we had ever seen.

Todd and I crouched on our knees, filtering the contents of the sand for the best nugget we could find. We bounced around like prizefighters, limbering our muscles for the big duel, each convinced we could outpitch the other. Even weeks of practice proved no advantage, as the raging rapids greedily swallowed our stones.

"Hey, I dare you to swim to the other side," Charles said, glaring at me. The brisk air was empowering. "Bet you can't do it."

"Oh, yeah?" I replied, guessing that the river was easily forty feet at its deepest point.

"I double dare you," he retorted.

"Wanna bet?" I heard myself answer, thinking I might as well make a little cash in the process.

"How about lunch money?" he suggested. "Whaddaya think, Todd?"

"Sounds good to me," Todd said, relieved to be gambling instead of swimming.

Without a second thought, I stripped down to my boxers and flung both pants and shirt on the riverbank. Mentally surveying the course, I chose the sandbar—a safe spot to touch bottom and catch my breath—as my first goal. After all, I was a strong swimmer. This was going to be easy money.

The water was colder than I had anticipated, as I jumped right in. Initially, the current's sheer strength gave my arms and legs a steady workout. This might, I reasoned, be harder than I thought. After several minutes of fighting the current, I was grateful to find a short log. Its rough surface cradled my head like a pillow. It felt good to rest. Just one more moment before I would release the log and swim to the bank in record time. I turned my head to adjust the angle of the wood and could hardly digest the sight before me. My entire body froze, as I came nose to nose with a long, black water moccasin. Our eyes locked, but I had no plans to outstare him. Recharged, I found the energy to conquer the current and put some distance between us. I desperately searched for a safe destination, all the while knowing that I was no match for the serpent's deadly venom and aquatic skill.

Escaping into the open current, I was finally free of the snake. Or so I thought. Inches away, I spotted a thinner, more brightly colored snake—a copperhead—deftly making his move. Gliding into the water from a smaller piece of driftwood, he headed in my direction, and to my horror, he was not alone. In fact, snakes lurked everywhere. At first, I guessed that there must be a handful; however, my estimate turned to dozens, or maybe a hundred in all—water moccasins and copperheads, but also rattlesnakes—in different sizes. Apparently, they also thought it was a nice day for a swim.

I heard Charles and Todd screaming wildly, and I figured that I was already off course by at least five hundred yards. I was also convinced that they would probably never see me alive again. We would never cheer the same victories or second-guess the same defeats. Daddy always said that a snakebite was an easy death. Holding onto that thought, I told God that I was prepared to die.

Somehow, I found the resolve to keep swimming. Instinctively I changed directions and set my course for another bank. The force of the current became even stronger as it passed over the sandbar, but I was not concentrating on the water's relentless tug. My only goal was to outswim the army of snakes in time to reach the water's edge.

Without warning, my body was once again swept away by the current. I employed every ounce of strength to finally reach the channel of the river—my safety net. My friends rushed to greet me at the shore, each grabbing one of my slippery hands to yank me from the water.

"Wow! That was some swimming!" Charles shouted.

"Man, we thought you were a goner," Todd barked. His short, blondish brown hair was slick with perspiration.

"Have you ever seen so many snakes?" I screeched, still panting from my ordeal. I collapsed on dry land, never feeling a finer bed. The blue sky looked bluer than a robin's egg, and the air smelled sweeter than a Sunday dinner.

"Snakes?" they answered in unison. Both swore that they didn't see any such reptiles. In fact, they had only seen my frenzied attempts to wrestle the mighty Tyronza.

Without hesitation, Charles and Todd each surrendered fifteen cents as payment for a hard-won dare. I pocketed my winnings, and it was clearly the toughest money I had ever earned.

Looking back, I think an angel must have been sitting on my shoulder. God allowed me to live and welcome my new baby sister, Carolyn, who arrived a few weeks later.

8.

Other seasons brought other escapades, some of which are better forgotten. One such adventure occurred in early 1949, when Parkin found itself in the middle of a hard winter. The brutal January wind shrieked throughout the night, and we awakened to find the frozen ground blanketed by snow. For us kids, the first fall of powdery white stuff was nature's invitation to play outdoors. For at least one fourth grader, this was not the case. My only pair of shoes, soaked clear through the soles from the walk home the day before, had been left too close to the kerosene heater and had burned to ashes.

No one needed to remind me that September was the only month that we got new shoes—high-top, lace-up broughams—or that my pair was expected to last a full year. How could I let this happen? I had always taken such good care of my shoes, prolonging their lives with cardboard until the soles were so thin that I could step on a dime and tell whether it was heads or tails. With this pair destroyed, even fresh cardboard wouldn't help.

"But I can't go to school tomorrow," I pleaded over and over to my father. "I don't have any shoes, and my feet will freeze."

"You're going to school, shoes or no shoes," he shouted above my protests. Once Daddy's mind was made up, I knew it was useless to raise the issue again. While I dreaded the impossible trek to school, the very idea of walking into the classroom with bare feet was even worse.

Mama gave me an extra hug the next morning as I set out on the longest two miles of my young life. In the bitter cold, I struggled to keep up with Jimmy and Bobbie. It didn't take long for my feet to throb in pain from the wet and cold. Gradually, the sharp ache gave way to numbness. My knees buckled to force one foot in front of the other. I knew that any physical discomfort would pale in comparison to the embarrassment to come. Although my friends were also poor, at least they would be wearing shoes.

Sure enough, I stumbled into the classroom, nearly frozen and out of breath. Aware that nothing could hide my predicament, I located my desk and attempted to act as if nothing were wrong. A predictable gasp radiated around the room. I wanted so badly to explain what happened. Maybe they would understand, I hoped. Instead, someone called out: "Hey, Jackie, where are your shoes?"

Laughter broke out before I could answer. I felt a million eyes watching, as my classmates snickered among themselves. Imagining what they were whispering to each other was worse than knowing. Very few even spoke directly to me, which was just as well. I fought the urge to cry as my feet slowly thawed.

The numbness subsided by recess, and I hoped that my teacher would let me stay in the classroom. To add insult to injury, she ordered me to the playground. I knew it was her first year to teach in Parkin, so she might be afraid to break the rules. Just this once, I wanted to be the exception. My feet were purple.

"Please," I begged, hugging the radiator. "It's freezing out there. I won't be any trouble. My shoes burned up."

"Sorry," she cut me off. I watched as she pulled a heavy, wool sweater from the back of her chair and wrapped it around her shoulders. "You'll have to go outside, like everyone else." That was that.

The rest of the day I was too humiliated to keep my mind on our daily lessons. As soon as school was finished, I hobbled home.

When Saturday rolled around, Daddy agreed to take me shopping. At last, I could cover my feet and gain back some dignity. I was determined to be more careful next time. I was even more determined that if I ever got caught in that situation again, I would have enough money to buy myself some shoes. Going to class barefoot in cold weather was an experience that I'll never forget. Today, I buy each of my grandchildren a new pair of shoes at the start of every school year.

The shoe episode not only hurt my pride, but it also put a crimp in my social life. From that time forward, none of the girls wanted anything to do with me.

By February 14, 1950, Valentine's Day, the snow had melted, and the sun was shining. Our walk to school was definitely easier. That day my heart beat a bit stronger than usual. Sandwiched between my books was a handful of red and white Valentines, purchased with hard-saved pennies for classmates whom I considered special. I could hardly wait to deliver my cards at the appointed time.

The room was buzzing as I opened the door. We all knew that it would be early afternoon by the time our teacher gave permission to begin the annual exchange. After lunch, she made the big announcement. I quickly passed out my Valentines and returned to my seat, anxious to receive and open those addressed to me. My friends giggled as they scurried back and forth. I held my breath as each girl brushed by my desk, but no one handed me an envelope. Again and again, my hopes rose, only to fall in the next second. Once everyone was seated, my heart sank. The hurt, which I had thought was long gone, went from bad to worse. I realized that no one had given me a Valentine. For me, the happiest part of the day was when it ended.

9.

By the time I was a decade old, I knew that filling a need for others could result in cash. No wonder I was always on the prowl for business opportunities.

To my delight, I discovered that fishermen would pay a penny apiece for bait, specifically cockroaches. The demand was particularly great when fish spawned in the spring, because "shellcrackers"—fish that were part of the brim family—favored roaches. Although others might not find roaches attractive, I wasn't afraid to capture the critters in bulk. After all, it was easy to envision each one as a shiny penny just waiting to be earned. To start this enterprise, I devised a special trap, consisting of a mesh wire box with a rolled wire, funnel-shaped opening.

My bait business was launched behind the grocery store alley, clearly the best roach-hunting spot in town. Meticulously, I placed my prey's favorite food, a banana peel, inside the contraption and watched the bugs march inside. Once a roach entered the box, it could not escape. On a good day, an hour netted at least one or two hundred little prisoners. It wasn't long before local anglers became loyal customers. Each night, I arrived home one or two dollars richer.

Once the mercury inched south, I visited neighbors to ask permission to pick pecans on the halves from their land. Pecan trees grew wild in our part of the country, and the industrious squirrels were my only competition. I cut a deal with several property owners, and we each kept half of the profits.

Proving that one man's trash is another man's treasure, I also collected discarded scrap iron, including copper and aluminum, to sell to a dealer in town. In addition, wire coat hangers, gathered from residents who no longer wanted them, were exchanged for two cents each. Coke bottles—for that matter, any soda and water bottles—could be redeemed for two cents apiece. These side jobs had little or no start-up costs and produced free money.

By the time I was eleven years old, I could easily pick two hundred pounds of cotton a day as good as, if not better than, most men. Our neighbors expected that I would follow in my parents' footsteps, but deep inside, I knew that there had to be a better way to make a living. I longed to see and experience the world beyond Parkin, a dream that only money and education could fuel. Sometimes, my resourceful ways also caught the attention of other adults who needed a job done.

"Jackie, Mr. Kelly will pay three dollars a day to chop cotton in his fields," my mother told me one Friday morning in July. "He says the work should take about a week. It's okay with us if you're interested, but you still have to keep up with your chores around here."

Interested? I could hardly believe my ears. Money was so scarce that I jumped at Mr. Kelly's proposition. I had no illusions about the long days—perhaps twelve hours or more, sunup to sundown—but I didn't complain.

On Monday morning, I arrived at work just before dawn and discovered that Mr. Kelly's fields were choked with overgrown weeds.

The assignment looked much harder than I had bargained for, but I was determined to keep my word.

I began to hack away at the cotton, bit by bit, quietly focused on what seemed like a near-impossible job at hand. For hours on end, I swung the chopping hoe back and forth, back and forth, until every muscle in my body ached to quit. After several rows, I retrieved a file from my pocket, then hit the blade a couple of times to keep it sharp. Years earlier, I had mastered the art of putting a fine edge on a hoe. Although I despised sharecropping, I strived for perfection and efficiency. I repeated the steps, row by row, day in and day out. I mentally broke the task into smaller portions, so that my goal seemed easier to reach. Every day at noon, I searched for a patch of shade to eat my lunch and seek relief from the sizzling heat, which now hovered around one hundred degrees. The highlight of my routine was when I ate the lunch that Mama had packed. Usually my lunch was a peanut butter sandwich topped with jelly, or if I was really lucky, slices of banana.

"Hey, Little Pa Shaw," my neighbors called out, waving as they passed by. I returned their greeting, waving the straw hat that earned me that nickname after my grandfather.

By the third day, even smiling had become an effort. I had bent over at least a million times in the blistering heat. My hands were raw from the repetition of chopping a difficult field, and every patch of my exposed skin was sunburned.

Just before the sun slipped out of sight on Friday evening, my endeavor was complete. I looked over the field and felt enormously proud. The monstrous undertaking was finished on schedule. Even better, I had done a fine job.

Saturday morning was payday. I was glad when Mr. Kelly and his foreman arrived in a dusty, black pick-up truck to survey my accomplishment. Finally, all of my hard work would be rewarded.

To my dismay, his reaction was the opposite of what I had expected. "You call this a good job?" he asked defiantly.

"Yes, sir!" I blurted out, caught off guard that he would even suggest otherwise.

"Jackie, this is not at all what I asked you to do," he said. His eyes narrowed as he rubbed a patch of whiskers, embedded in his wrinkled cheek. "Half the work gets half the pay."

I thought of how many hours I had labored among the cotton plants that were in much worse condition than he had described. "No, you're going to pay me the full amount," I fired back. "Look, I've done a good job chopping your cotton. If you didn't like the way I was doing it, you should have told me right away, not let me work all week."

I could feel my heart pounding like a hammer, but I stood my ground, staring him straight in the eye. His mouth popped open like a flycatcher. I was furious that he would try to cheat on our deal. It was the first time someone in business had attempted to take advantage of me. The minutes passed like hours, but I was not backing down, and he knew it. In disbelief, Mr. Kelly turned to his foreman.

"Can you believe what just came out of that boy's mouth?" he asked.

"I do, and I think you better give the boy his money," the foreman said. A pregnant pause hung in the air.

Reluctantly, Mr. Kelly reached in his pocket and fumbled around for fifteen dollars. "Here," he grumbled. "Take it."

10.

Every Sunday evening when the weather permitted, Parkin's downtown dirt diamond came alive with America's favorite pastime. Young players itched to take their turns on base. Grown-ups played until they could hardly walk. Simply put, baseball was revered.

At twelve years old, I was a Little League veteran, savoring my fifth season of play. My claim to fame was that I was both the captain and the star catcher of the Parkin Tigers. On an overcast day in June, we were vying for the division championship. I woke up confident and raring to win. Before I left for the big game, Mama reminded me of a chore yet to be finished. Even sports stars could not escape the reality of routine.

"Don't forget to pick those peaches," she yelled, as I headed out the door. "The ones near the top of the barn are ripe."

With my mind more on events to come than on the job at hand, I scampered up on the tin roof to harvest the plump, flesh-colored fruit. My pitching hand was poised for plucking, when big raindrops pelted the metal beneath me. As the drops fell faster, the roof's rippled surface turned slippery. I had no choice but to grasp the edge of the metal, squatting and leaning forward to stay afoot. Gravity had other plans. Helpless to stop my body from sliding, I flinched as the cold, rusty metal sliced my index finger almost to the bone. By the time my body fell to the ground, blood was everywhere. *Of all days,* I thought. The physical pain was secondary to the desperation I felt in letting my team down. *Today, defeat is not an option*, I reasoned, *even if my finger falls off.*

A couple of hours later, I found myself standing in front of Coach Kemp, facing the biggest game of the season. "Ready, guys?" he asked in his most chipper tone. We nodded in unison. Standing six feet tall with dark hair parted in the middle, Cecil Kemp physically resembled box-office star Jack Lemmon. Exhibiting a no-nonsense confidence, he was our ultimate role model—a rugged and highly disciplined guy who took to coaching like a duck to water.

Concealed beneath a much-weathered glove, my finger reminded me of its injury every time I threw the ball. By the top of the fifth inning, I cautiously peeled off the mitt to relieve the pressure. Now bloody, the bandage that Mama had so carefully wrapped caught the attention of Jimmy Wooten's mother, who motioned to me from the bleachers. Mrs. Wooten was easy to spot, thanks to her multicolored shirtdress. Prior to the season, I had only known this tall, feisty woman in passing. Her husband owned the local Pontiac dealership, and Jimmy's family always had a new car. Thanks to baseball, I had grown to trust her generous nature.

"Here, Jackie," Mrs. Wooten said, forcing two aspirin tablets into my throbbing hand. "Take these. You'll feel better."

Even though I had never taken aspirin before, I agreed and forced a smile. Her kindness had also drawn the interest of Coach Kemp. Unfortunately, he was not the only one who took notice. When the game resumed, our opponents wasted no time in stealing bases, fully aware that I was not playing with my usual dexterity. Our perceptive leader instructed me to swap positions for the outfield. My replacement couldn't pitch the ball, and our jaws collectively dropped, as we started to fall behind.

"If you boys win the game, I'll buy hamburgers for everyone," Daddy said, when he stopped by the dugout.

"Really?" I asked, amazed that my father would make such an extravagant promise.

"You bet," he said, grinning ear to ear.

"Hey, Coach, put me back in," I pleaded.

"I can't, Jackie," he said. "You're hurt."

"Please, please," I said. "It's my decision. Please."

Coach Kemp nodded as I reclaimed my turf, buoyed by a drive to win at all costs. *This old boy is going to steal on me,* I thought, sensing movement from third base. With all of my might, I heaved the ball. He was out, but the play blew my finger wide open. No matter. Nothing could dampen my enthusiasm or that of the fans, who were now standing and cheering at the top of their lungs.

By the bottom of the seventh inning, bases were loaded, and the Parkin Tigers had two outs. Undaunted, I drew a deep breath and amazed myself by hitting a triple. The ball almost cleared the fence as I sailed around the bases on pure adrenaline.

"You can stop right there," Coach Kemp triumphantly informed me at third base. "We have enough runs to win the game."

That day, I knew how Babe Ruth must have felt. The roar of the crowd said it all. In the euphoria of the moment, I searched for my father. So did my coach. Vying for victory, the team had worked up an appetite, and we were ready to party. Daddy, however, was nowhere to be found. Apparently his alligator mouth had overloaded his mosquito butt.

11.

One promise Daddy did keep was moving our family away from Parkin for a better life. By January of 1952, my parents were fed up with sharecropping and were ready for a change. My father sought employment in Crawfordsville. The bustling town with a population of six hundred was only twenty miles east, but it might as well have been in the next state. None of us kids had ever been that far away.

"Hurry up, Opal!" Daddy called impatiently to Mama. It was moving day. He gunned the motor, and I prayed that his fiery temper would not explode. Please God, not today.

Mama must have been praying, too. Climbing inside the car, she sighed and wiped her eyes. There was a knowing silence as the vehicle pulled away from the house where I was born. Crammed with my siblings in the back seat, I dared to imagine the future in our new home. Even my usually noisy brother and sisters were silent as we puttered down the dirt road, craning our necks for one last look.

I tried to memorize the familiar sights that I had always taken for granted, not knowing when, or even if, I would ever pass through

Parkin again. My head was dizzy, just mulling over my first dozen years. Not all my recollections were good, but even so, I felt a little sad. It was a struggle to put on a brave face. I thought of the countless times I'd heard Mama and Daddy arguing through the night. My mind drifted to swimming in the river, walking barefoot to school, hitting the home run as a Parkin Tiger, and suddenly I saw a sweet image of Billy Ray. How could he be laughing one day and gone the next? Yes, Crawfordsville, I reasoned, had to be better.

Once on the main road, there was no turning back. We began to reminisce as we shuffled our bodies in the back of our dark blue Chevrolet, heaped high with all the stuff we deemed important. At long last, we were taking a step in the right direction. I began to feel excited, even exuberant, as the bitter wind sandpapered our faces. We passed other farms with barren fields and idle equipment just waiting for spring. Knowing that my parents would not be sharecropping gave me a profound sense of relief.

Within the hour, Daddy turned down a gravel road. In the distance, we spotted a white frame house with a brick veneer.

"Hey, kids, that's our home!" Mama shouted.

The house, she explained, was owned by Daddy's new employer, the Bloodworth family. From previous conversations, I knew that they owned the Gulf service station that my father would operate.

"Guess what? It has indoor plumbing," Mama added. "No heat, but indoor plumbing." The vehicle rocked with cheers and applause. This was already a big improvement.

Before long, Mama opened a little restaurant she named Opal's Café. With luck, she found a building in downtown Crawfordsville that had been constructed with a restaurant in mind. The owner was generous enough to let Mama rent from him, and she took enormous pride in her venture, which boasted six barstools and three booths. If all of the customers had been strapped inside, Opal's Café had enough room for about twenty diners.

Thanks to a prime location next door to the bank and Mama's hard work, her undertaking became quite successful. Opal's Café opened at 6 and offered a full breakfast. Customers could order a plate lunch at noon with a choice of two meats—roast beef and chicken, pork, or meatloaf—and three vegetables. Mama's dessert menu consisted of her homemade lemon, chocolate, and coconut pies, as well as fresh fried fruit pies served with ice cream. At dinner, patrons could choose from a full line of sandwiches and hamburgers with soft drinks and fries. Steaks were also available, although not too many people could afford steaks back then. The restaurant closed at 10.

It was a long day for Mama, but she loved owning and operating her own business. As far as I could tell, her job presented only one major obstacle: transportation. Now that my parents worked in separate areas, a single vehicle was hard to share. Because we lived out in the country instead of in town, I was also isolated, and at first, I had a lot of idle time. One day I had a brainstorm.

"I can drive," I told Daddy.

"Jackie, you don't know how to drive," he said.

"Yes, sir, I do," I told him.

"You can drive?" he asked. "Who taught you how?"

Jimmy had let me drive our old truck a couple of times. Other times, I took mental notes of what he did.

"I think Jimmy showed me," I said. "I know I can drive."

"Well, then, you're going to take me to work," he said.

Early the next morning, I drove Daddy to work and discovered that there wasn't much difference between driving a truck and a car. When we pulled into the service station, my father was obviously tickled.

"You think you can go home and take your mother to work?" he asked.

I drove about three miles north of town to our house, picked up Mama, and delivered her to Opal's Café. After that, my parents let me use the car regularly, and I got to know my way around town. My own transportation to eighth grade was by school bus.

Before we moved from Parkin, I had been tapped as an official member of the Little League state team. To my great disappointment, there was no baseball team at my new school. As the new kid in town, I had no reputation and worried about fitting in. No doubt, I felt a little anxious about making friends and finding my place among others who had grown up together. Happily, the ride to and from school forged friendships with two regular riders: Jimmy Currie and John Paul (who preferred "Paul") Sorrel. Both boys had gawky, basketball player physiques and were grade levels ahead of me—Jimmy, by three years and Paul, by two—yet, it was not book learning that drew us together. We all loved to hunt and fish. In our spare time, the three of us could be found stalking prey in the thick woods that surrounded Crawfordsville.

Shotgun shells were expensive—three for twenty-five cents—so by necessity, we prudently calculated our shots. This habit produced two-fold benefits. It made our trips more affordable and encouraged us to be better hunters. Small wonder that even with snow on the ground, we were accused of tracking rabbits until they just quit running. Jimmy, Paul, and I also agreed on eating or using everything we killed or caught. We practiced conservation years before it became popular.

Paul and I also had something else in common. Most of the boys in his family had been sharecroppers; we both related to that lifestyle, and knew what it was like to be poor. We lived by the old adage: "If one buys the wine, you can't afford the bread." Compared to us, Jimmy was well off, but he never bragged about his status. In fact, he and his family were kind enough to share their resources with us. I especially liked his thoughtful mother, who always packed plenty of sandwiches for our expeditions and routinely welcomed us home with a hot meal.

12.

As a bigger town experiencing growing pains, Crawfordsville offered more opportunities. For starters, Crawfordsville High School, which actually included grades one through twelve, was tops in the district. Although I was impressed by my new school, employment possibilities were equally important.

"If you want to work at Griffin Grocery, they have a job open," my brother mentioned to me over breakfast one Saturday.

"How do you know?" I asked.

"'Cause they offered it to me," he said.

"Why didn't you take it?" I persisted, suspecting the real reason for Jimmy's reluctance was that he didn't care much for work.

"No reason in particular," he said. "Just wasn't interested."

"Well, if you don't want the job, I do!" I said, springing from the kitchen table. I was out the door in a flash, heading to the largest grocery store in town.

Once there, I introduced myself to Dan Griffin, who managed the store with his wife, Jane. Both worked for the owners, Cliff and Catherine Britton, a young, well-to-do couple. The pride in their establishment was evident, and I was already enamored with the idea of working at Griffin Grocery. Its clean, well-organized shelves and easy-to-navigate aisles far outshone any store that I had ever visited. Never before had I seen so many types of food displayed in one place!

"I understand you're looking to hire some help," I said, overcoming my initial awe.

"How old are you, son?" Mr. Griffin asked, obviously amused. He shook my hand firmly and untied his long, white butcher's apron, stained with raw meat drippings. With dark brown hair and a mature, friendly face, I surmised he was around thirty years my senior. "We were actually looking for someone older with a driver's license," he said. I detected a hint of disappointment.

"I'm thirteen, but I've got experience," I explained, standing as straight as possible, "and I've been driving since I was ten."

"Really?" he said. I could tell he was interested but not convinced. Undeterred, I began to sell the product I knew best—myself. By the end of my pitch, it was obvious that Dan Griffin had met the right person for the job. His wife nodded optimistically, and I hoped that her encouragement would seal the deal.

"Can you start tomorrow?" he asked, leaning forward.

"You bet!" I replied, without hesitation. Life in Crawfordsville was good. I had landed my first regular job.

As soon as school dismissed on weekdays, I reported to the store to make deliveries that were called in during the day. In short order, I learned the customers' names and grocery preferences. It didn't take long for me to become the fair-haired delivery boy. Many of these customers were not home when I delivered their orders, yet they thought nothing of leaving a key for me to go inside and put away their purchases.

I earned two dollars every weekday afternoon, and on Saturday, the biggest day in the grocery business, my pay was six dollars for working from 7 in the morning to midnight. Trying to balance work with school was not an easy feat, but I was determined to succeed.

Although there were five food stores in town, Griffin Grocery was the most popular. Located on Main Street across from Rexall Drugs, which was renowned for its frosty cherry limeades, the yellow brick establishment was a hive of activity. Every time I walked through the screen doors, I felt like smiling right back at the colorful Rainbo Bread kids, whose faces were immortalized on the attached metal signs.

I ate, lived, and breathed Griffin Grocery, reveling in the friendly atmosphere and pure buzz of commerce. I memorized every item contained inside its four thousand square feet, from fresh tomatoes and dairy products to lard by the stand, flour by the barrel, and half-barrel, and kerosene. During that time, Sara Lee, a new line of convenience foods, was earning the endorsement of customers with ready-made cheesecake, pound cake, and Danish rolls.

The daughter of a former mayor, Mrs. Griffin had been raised in Crawfordsville and knew everyone. Under her watchful eye, I mastered each job the store required to operate efficiently, including butchering and cutting meat, which was previously Mr. Griffin's domain. There I was, the poorest kid in town, but the owners gave me their vote of confidence and trusted me with a great deal of responsibility. Our relationship was more than employee-employer. We were a team. The Griffins became close friends, and I took great pride in putting forth my best effort.

Getting to know the shoppers was a side benefit of my employment. Although the Brittons were the landlords, they had nothing to do with the day-to-day operation of Griffin Grocery. Catherine Britton was, however, one of our best customers.

With her keen fashion sense, green eyes, and short, sandy brown hair, Mrs. Britton was the type of woman that men referred to as the cat's meow. Make no mistake; she was a true lady, who took her role as a wife, mother, and friend seriously. When Mr. Griffin introduced us, I was doubly impressed by the charm and style of a true Southern belle.

"Please, just call me Cooter," she said, extending her hand. I had never met such an elegant individual. I later learned that her grandfather was the town's founder.

So began our friendship. Once a week, I delivered a case of six and one-half ounce Coca-Colas to Cooter, who I preferred to call Miss Catherine. Retrieving the empty, returnable glass bottles from customers was my least favorite job, but I never dreaded the stop at Miss Catherine's. Many times she could be found pruning azaleas or digging in her garden, and she was always wearing a dress, hat, and gloves. It was clear that Miss Catherine loved the land as much as Scarlett O'Hara loved Tara. Even so, she usually insisted on taking a break and inviting me to join her for a cool drink.

Our relationship grew to include invitations on Sunday afternoons when her husband and son were not at home. In fact, I was expected to drop by. Miss Catherine was a skilled conversationalist, but during these visits, I discovered her greatest asset was listening. She worded the conversation so that I would elaborate, and she seemed to sense when I had a problem. Over time, Miss Catherine became my cheerleader. She encouraged me, not only in school, but also in life. When I was down, her kind words picked me up. If I did something foolish, she brought me back to reality. Even with the demands of a young son, Miss Catherine cleared time to make a difference in my life. We never grew tired of talking with each other.

Miss Catherine's actions also taught me to believe in myself. She had many great friends, but she didn't really care what people thought about her. She was definitely her own person, and everybody respected her.

The wheels in my head were always turning, concocting additional ways to make money. Thanks to the loan of the Griffins' truck, Sunday was also my day to be a businessman. Timing was everything. After church, I changed into my overalls, taking care to fasten only one button, and drove to the farmers' market in nearby Memphis to shop around. I knew exactly what items to buy and didn't have much time to compare prices. By early afternoon, vendors from the Rio Grande Valley were ready to sell their goods and head home. I, of course, was pleased to oblige. Customers were waiting in Crawfordsville.

"Watermelon?" I harked, traveling door to door with a sample of the green-striped produce tucked like a football under my arm. I felt smug to have purchased summer's favorite fruit for a quarter each and even more smug to double my investment."What else you got there, Jackie?" became music to my ears.

"Cantaloupes sweet as sugar," I proudly declared, motioning toward the truck. At the beginning of the route, my inventory included eight to ten bushels of cantaloupes. I paid only two dollars and fifty cents per bushel, but my cash outlay quadrupled by day's end.

"Eggs still warm, only fifty cents," I added, having discovered that people bought fresh eggs when they wouldn't buy anything else. Again, I only paid a quarter a dozen for brown or "yard" eggs.

The thrill of closing a sale—the game of bargaining and negotiating, then buying and selling—proved a source of entertainment as well as profit. I loved that the fruits of my labor went directly to me. By Sunday evening, my pockets were full.

13.

I had worked long enough that I knew not to get complacent. My mind churned with new ideas, and I seized every opportunity to make a nickel. In addition to working at Griffin Grocery and selling produce on my own, I cleaned the bank, sweeping, mopping, and dusting to perfection, for one dollar a day. I undertook this job between 5 and 6 on weekdays before school. When my friends and I planned a hunting trip, the bank got scoured from one to two in the morning. During these hours, I was the only one in the bank, but I was never lonely or scared.

It was about this time that I found myself keenly interested in the difference between boys and girls. With both hormones and curiosity running wild, I finally mustered the courage to ask a classmate for a date. Needless to say, my heart nearly burst when the object of my affection—a sweet but plain brunette somewhat taller than I was—answered affirmatively and asked me to be at her house by 6 on Sunday evening

All day long, I pondered our encounter. My nerves were overcome with questions about this big deal known as romance. As the designated hour approached, I combed my hair and dressed in my fanciest go-to-church clothes.

Although northeastern Arkansas was rural, the location of my date's house seemed especially remote. Concealed from the main road in a heavily forested area commonly known as the "sticks," the wood-frame home and adjacent property appeared creepy and dark. I still remember the ominous groan of the motor as I pulled to a stop. Heaving a deep breath, I started the long walk to her front door. At long last, love.

"There he is! Shoot him!" a raspy voice hollered.

Terrified, I squinted as a spotlight blinded me. I was scared to death that my own demise was mere seconds away. Naturally, my gut reaction was to run, but my little legs froze. *If this is romance, I don't want to get involved*, I thought. *It's just too much to bear.* In that single moment, I didn't care if I ever saw another girl.

When my legs finally moved and carried me to Daddy's '39 Ford truck, the engine wouldn't start. Once again, unable to budge and paralyzed with fear, I prayed that my life would be spared. After what felt like an eternity, the motor turned over, and I didn't look back. I was more scared that night than when I swam with snakes. Even though I survived, the ordeal took a dozen years off my life. Later, I found out that my sweetheart's entire family was involved in the joke. I was just glad to get out of those woods alive.

In time, I overcame the humiliation of my first date—the one that never really happened—and asked another girl out. I was only thirteen years old when I hid a bottle of red wine in the car and composed a little rhyme to boost my confidence:

> I bought a bottle of Thunderbird wine,
> What was the reason?
> It was the season.
> What was the price?
> Thirsty twice.

Maybe, I reasoned, a sip of wine would add to the romance. That night, I got cold feet and never opened the bottle. Even though that date was an improvement over the first, it wasn't in the cards for me to have a steady girlfriend. Unlike Miss Catherine and Miss Jane, who saw my potential, no adults wanted their daughters involved with the likes of me. To them, I was bad news, the dirt of the earth. I had no money, and therefore, no future to offer.

Once, the father of a girl I liked even bribed me to end our relationship. "I'll give you five dollars a month to quit dating my daughter," he said.

"I need money, but I think I'll pass on yours," I told him. "You don't need to spell it out. I won't come around anymore."

To this day, I never told that girl about her father's suggestion. I might not have been rich, but I had my standards.

14.

From the time I was a little boy, I attended church services. My grandfather built First Baptist Church of Parkin, and, over the years, I developed a real love of going to church for the right reason. Like many other small Arkansas towns, Crawfordsville had three denominations. For two years, I accompanied Miss Catherine and Miss Jane to the Methodist Church and went to Catholic Mass—then celebrated in Latin—with Jimmy Currie. Through these services, I gained a greater understanding and comfort level about other denominations. My roots, however, were Baptist, so First Baptist Church of Crawfordsville was the place I chose to officially proclaim my faith.

You always knew July had arrived in Crawfordsville when the Baptist church held a rousing revival. It was in the middle of such a celebration that Paul and I opted to accept Jesus Christ as our savior. At the age of fourteen, just knowing I was about to do something right for my soul was a wonderful feeling. I looked forward to this moving time of fellowship, music, and preaching with unbridled enthusiasm. An inspirational event in the buckle of the Bible Belt was guaranteed to draw a crowd.

The service attracted people of all backgrounds, including those who might not usually be seen around the premises on Sunday mornings. Unlike others, who waited for the right moment to be stirred, Paul and I made a pact in advance. After a couple of revival services, I knew the time for my spiritual birth had arrived. All week long, I pondered how this event would change my life.

"Paul, I'm going to walk down tonight," I informed my friend. "I feel it's the right thing to do." Paul agreed.

On the final night of the revival, the two of us entered the church with a newfound reverence, hungry to become part of something far greater. A glorious sight greeted us. At full capacity, the sanctuary comfortably held about seventy-five worshippers, but the turnout was definitely larger on this steamy summer evening. We pressed through the noisy crowd and found a couple of seats before the program got underway.

The service commenced with singing loud enough to shake the steeple. A handful of powerful testimonials followed. At last, the stately guest preacher strolled to the pulpit. He firmly grasped its sides before making eye contact with the crowd. The clergyman was at most, in his late thirties, but he had no trouble delivering a booming fire and brimstone sermon that Charlton Heston would envy. In fact, the minister made us feel that if we didn't get on the train, we would be left behind and lose our chance at salvation.

The invitation was issued. Paul and I traded brave glances, gulped, and walked down the center aisle to answer our calling. We were not the only ones. We found ourselves surrounded by believers of all backgrounds, including many other teenagers. As if on cue, the stained glass windows, a mosaic rainbow of color by day, darkened with nightfall, lending an even more solemn tone to this wondrous occasion.

Slowly, in unison, we approached the altar. It looked even bigger and brighter up close, but I was not afraid. After mopping his receding hairline, our pastor, Brother Rowe, placed his hands on my head. I felt the good Lord himself welcome me into a new life as I was immersed in the water of the baptistery tank. I surfaced, relieved, dripping wet, and gasping for air. Without question, I felt absolutely eaten up with the spirit. I felt brand new, like my life had fresh meaning and purpose. I was so energized by the experience that I ran home. Like my triple, when the Parkin Tigers won the division championship, I never felt my feet touch the ground.

To my knowledge, I was the first one in my immediate family to be saved. Although my parents never took us to church, I was glad that my grandparents had. It's interesting that even though Mama, Daddy, Jimmy, and my sisters did not attend services with me or even comprehend the importance of what happened in my life that night, they seemed pleased at my actions.

Now that it was official, my decision not to question the particulars was reinforced to a greater extent. Back in Parkin, I attended Sunday school and was taught that Adam and Eve were the first two people on earth; however, in elementary school, we learned Darwin's theory of evolution. The funny thing is that I had the same teacher for both classes.

"I'm a little confused," I remember telling Mrs. Bell, "so I'm just going to give the good Lord credit for whatever happened."

15.

My faith was tested sooner rather than later. In November of that year, I found myself with a group of friends heading to the hospital in Memphis. The night before, Jimmy was diagnosed with polio. My mind struggled to digest the news before we reached his bedside. It all seemed surreal. I'd never personally known anyone with polio, and now it happened to be one of my best friends.

Even more strange was that it was Jimmy, who had been the picture of health, who was the victim. At six feet, nine inches, he was the tallest kid in school and hard to miss in a crowd. Until the day before, Jimmy's biggest issue had been getting his thick, curly brown hair to comb straight. I thought he should save his money, since all the stuff he bought never worked. Besides, girls liked guys with curls.

The miles were a blur, as I gazed out the car window. I thought of how rapidly the disease attacked Jimmy, almost as if it were hunting him down. How weird that one day he felt great, and the next day he had a fever, followed by stiffness in his back and neck. For years, we'd heard horror stories about the dreaded disease that struck thousands every summer and fall. Newspaper photos of boys and girls confined to wheelchairs or, even worse, encased in iron lungs came to mind, even though I understood there were many degrees of polio. I worried that Jimmy might never be able to hunt and fish with us again. Even more, I worried about saying the wrong thing when I was with him.

All too soon we arrived at the hospital hoping to find reassurance in its whistle-clean halls and antiseptic smell. Surely something can be done to help Jimmy return to his old self, I prayed. The heavy glass doors swung open, and we sought directions at the front desk.

"I'm sorry, but visiting hours are over," said the nurse in charge.

"Aw, we've come all the way from Crawfordsville," said Buddy Sharp, the class comedian.

"I'm sorry," the nurse replied, adjusting her hat. "You're welcome to come back tomorrow." Without another word, she turned on her heel and walked around the corner.

Buddy was not about to give up. "How about that?" he asked. "We drove all the way here and can't even see Jimmy."

"You heard what she said," someone said. "Let's go."

"Wait," Buddy said, noticing a doctor's coat on a chair. "I have an idea." He donned the white lab coat, a near-perfect fit, and flung the attached stethoscope around his neck. We couldn't help but admire his resourcefulness. Thank goodness our laughter didn't arouse suspicion.

Our luck continued as we strolled down the halls and spotted Jimmy's older sister, Phoebe, standing outside his room. She was tall, although not as tall as Jimmy, and she was always soft-spoken.

"I'm so glad you've all come," Phoebe said in her sweet Southern drawl. She put on a brave front, but I could tell she had been crying.

Standing next to her, Mrs. Currie, usually so pretty and cheerful, looked drained. It was evident she was more than worried. Her eyes were tinged with red as they peered over reading glasses to greet us.

"How's Jimmy? Can we see him?" we took turns asking.

"He's very sick," she said, and calmly broke the news in detail. "The doctors tell us that Jimmy has acute flaccid paralysis. It's a form of polio that breaks down the muscles of his arms and legs."

"When will he get better?" I heard someone else ask. Normally a take-charge woman, Mrs. Currie shook her head and bit her lower lip.

Silently I thanked God that even though Jimmy's outlook was serious, at least he did not die. I closed my eyes and wondered if he wished he had. The very thought of my good friend having to rely on others to accomplish the business of everyday living was hard to fathom. I tried to wrap my mind around his helplessness and understand the long road he faced. In some small way, I was determined to help him live a normal life.

Slowly, Mrs. Currie opened the door to Jimmy's room, and our entourage paraded inside. For once, we were quiet, partly because Jimmy was sick and partly because Buddy's masquerade might be discovered by the hospital staff. To our surprise, Jimmy was unable to communicate. In fact, he was sleeping soundly, hooked up to every possible machine you could imagine. Clearly, his struggle was just beginning.

16.

Ducktails. Plaid shirts. Cool cars. In 1956, my friends and I were hypnotized by the beat of rock 'n' roll. When school was in session, a Friday night dance at the community hall, set to the cadence of 45-rpm records, became the highlight of our week. Although jitterbugging was not my specialty, I had no trouble keeping up with the latest sounds.

Whenever an upcoming concert was advertised, we piled into Jimmy's white Crown Victoria and hightailed it to Memphis. Jimmy's recovery had been long, slow, and draining, but after months of grueling treatment that included feeding tubes, heavy sedation, and a tracheotomy, the patient was deemed well enough to leave the hospital. Paul and I were determined to help our friend live as normal a life as possible, even if polio robbed him of the ability to walk. Equipped with braces, Jimmy was finally mobile. Even though his right leg was paralyzed, the limited use of his left leg allowed him to drive. At times, his life was almost normal.

Once in Memphis, we stood in line at the city auditorium, hoping to get tickets for a dollar or less. We marveled as the stage shook with the gyrations of Conway Twitty, The Platters, Jerry Lee Lewis, Fats Domino, Little Richard, Chubby Checker, Johnny Cash, The Drifters, Carl Perkins, and, of course the King, Elvis Presley.

By summer, the post-World War II housing boom provided gainful employment just twenty miles away in West Memphis. The pay was one dollar an hour, which was big money to a sixteen-year-old. I felt proud to be part of the construction labor force, earning some much-needed cash before embarking on my junior year of high school.

At home, there was an undercurrent of excitement. Around our tiny house, the mosquitoes and locusts were not the only ones buzzing. Mama seemed unusually jolly. I sensed an announcement was in the works.

My hunch was correct. Sweaty and bone tired, I barely closed the door behind me that steamy August afternoon when Mama called Patsy, Carolyn, and me into the kitchen. We sat quietly at the table as my world fell apart.

"Your daddy has taken a job in South Texas," Mama said. "We'll be moving there in a few weeks." Her words hung like thick molasses waiting to be stirred. By all accounts, I should have been ecstatic, but I felt like a baseball bat had landed squarely in my stomach.

Mama's eyes searched mine to see if I shared her joy. In her usual khaki pants and floral print shirt, she looked more energized and upbeat than she had in years. It was as if a great weight had been lifted from her shoulders. I knew Daddy was miserable in his work. Even though Mama's restaurant was successful and popular, it was clear that she was ready to move again. I tried my best to be positive, but the disappointment was too great to conceal. I thought of Paul, Jimmy, and all the friends I held dear. I thought of my church and my school. I ached for the life I would forever miss if I moved to Texas. Crawfordsville had been home for only four years, but it was the best home I'd ever had.

For the rest of the evening, I tried to reconcile my feelings. When my head hit the pillow, sleep was not automatic. Somewhere between darkness and daybreak, an idea surfaced. Earlier that year, Bobbie and her new husband had moved to Chicago. My older brother followed after he graduated in May. Both weren't much older than I was. Why couldn't I stay behind? After all, having one less mouth to feed would certainly help my parents. Trying to make it completely on my own would be just another challenge. Heaven knows that by now, I was used to challenges. I resolved not to move from Crawfordsville, at least until after high school.

When dawn broke, I was both anxious and reluctant to confront Mama. Once again, I found her in the kitchen, this time humming while she kneaded a stubborn mound of biscuit dough.

"I won't be going to Texas with you," I blurted out, without looking directly at her. "I've thought about moving, and I plan to stay here."

The silence between us was unbearable. I braced for a protest, but there was none. Finally, I mustered the nerve to lift my head. It was impossible to miss the hurt in her soft blue eyes. I never forgot that moment. All these years, my mother had been my angel, my rock. It upset me beyond words that we were parting this way, even though I knew that staying was the right choice for me.

Within days, I found myself bidding farewell as our car rumbled down the weed-lined driveway one last time, spurting swirls of dust as it transported my parents and younger sisters to the Lone Star State. All too soon, Mama and Daddy waved back through the open windows.

Pressing her hand to the rear windshield, Patsy wiped a wisp of light brown hair from her eyes as she fought back tears. I wondered how different seven-year-old Carolyn would look the next time we saw each other. She straightened her eyeglasses and stared first at me, then at Patsy. As the car disappeared in the distance, I felt all grown up and at peace with myself for sticking with a difficult decision. Things would be different now, I reasoned. I was on my own. Impulsively, I kicked a rock and wondered why I felt so sad.

That day at work, the hours passed more quickly than usual. I was grateful to be busy and surrounded by people, not having to think about my choice. As the sun melted into the horizon, the rest of the crew left for home. I deliberately shuffled and made excuses to stay behind until everyone was gone. Hungry and worn out, I walked a few yards to a small convenience store to buy Vienna sausage, crackers, and soda pop for supper. With nowhere to sleep, I returned to the job site and rummaged for some leftover water. The lukewarm liquid cooled my sunburned face and neck. Refreshed, I consumed my purchases slowly, savoring each morsel.

There's no denying that I was more alone and lonely than ever before. I was also scared. Exhausted from working in the grueling sun all day, I fought sleep as long as possible before the bright sky faded to purple. I surveyed the situation and decided to enter a partially bricked home, gathering stones for a bed and bricks for a pillow. Gradually I heard noises that were not audible during the day. In spite of my weariness, slumber did not come easily. For hours, I dozed on and off, wondering about my future. At long last, the sun—a welcome sight—crept into view.

I congratulated myself for surviving the long ordeal. That night was the first of thirty that I would spend at the construction site before returning to Crawfordsville. Many times I prayed for my safety and gradually got to know the Lord on a first-name basis. After all, we had the same initials. One evening, a transient also stopped to rest, and I didn't sleep the entire night. It was hard to tell which one of us was more afraid. The next day, we remedied the situation by introducing ourselves.

About three weeks later, I dodged a bullet.

"Hey Jackie, how come you're here at this time?" Startled, I turned around to see that my boss had arrived much earlier than usual.

"Just wanted to get to work on time, I guess," I casually replied, trying to conceal my homelessness. He had no clue where I had been sleeping night after night.

"Good for you!" he said, visibly impressed with my work ethic.

I learned there to expect an upside and a downside to everything. The upside of sleeping on the job site was that I was never late to work.

The earliest photo I have from my childhood was taken in summer of 1944. Caldwell kids pictured from the tallest to the smallest are: Jimmy, 8; Bobbie, 6; Jackie, 4; and Billy Ray, 3.

Age had its privileges and duties. Delivering water on horseback to Mama and Daddy in the cotton fields became one of my jobs when I turned five years old.

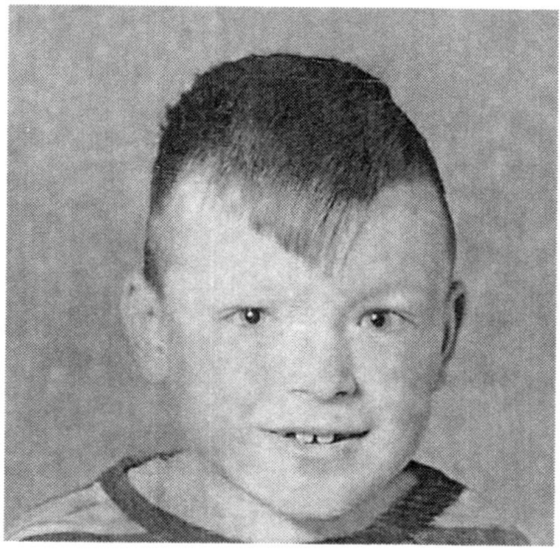

I was a proud first-grader with a bowl haircut in 1946.

My maternal grandfather, known to us as "Pa Shaw," had already fathered eight children by his first wife when the Mississippi widower met my grandmother. My mother, the oldest of his second eight children, shared his passion for hard work. Although not a large man, he was as strong as an ox.

Crawfordsville High School was the gateway to my future. I'll always be grateful to teachers who went the extra mile to prepare me for the real world. Built in 1913, the building burned to the ground in 1966 and was never rebuilt.

As a high school senior, I looked forward to attending Arkansas State in Jonesboro.

Cynthia was only 15 years old when my sister Patsy introduced us in summer of 1958.

Cynthia and I maintained a long-distance courtship for two years. This photo, taken at her junior-senior prom in 1960, is sometimes mistaken for our wedding photo. We married a few weeks later at the Harris County Courthouse in downtown Houston.

As newlyweds, Cynthia and I hammed it up in matching shirts.

From the very beginning, Cynthia and I were happy together. We needed no prompting for the camera in this 1961 snapshot when photo booths were the rage.

Cynthia and I celebrated our second Christmas together. Jack Jr., although not pictured, was four months old.

As evidenced by her corsage, it was a special day for Mama. Surrounding her (from left to right) were Daddy, Jimmy, me, Bobbie, Patsy, and Carolyn in 1965.

Here I am at 27 years of age, the father of two wonderful sons: Robert, 5, and Jack, 6. Don't we all look grown up in our suits?

My daughters, Lisa (left) and Amy (right) were as close in the mid 1970s as they are today. *(Photo by Olan Mills)*

A high school junior, my son Robert posed for his senior portrait in late spring of 1979. Tragically, a car crash claimed his life several weeks later. *(Photo by Lifetouch)*

We've come a long way since our childhood days in Arkansas, but my siblings and I still enjoy the opportunity to get together. (Left to right) Jimmy, Carolyn, Patsy and Bobbie joined the father of the bride in 1994 to celebrate the wedding of my daughter Lisa.

One of the joys of living in the Bayou City is the annual Houston Livestock Show and Rodeo. Cynthia and I were always ready to party in our western wear.

I'll never forget my Crawfordsville angels. Here I am in 2002, visiting with Catherine Britton (left) and Jane Griffin (right).

In a 2002 visit to Crawfordsville, John Paul Sorrel and I relived memories of high school with our former teacher Herman Philips and his wife Merle.

Our children blessed us with eight beautiful grandchildren.

By 2006, Cynthia's grueling treatment had taken its toll. Yet, she remained cheerful and positive even in her final days.

Cynthia really did save the last dance for me.

I am so proud of my children and their spouses:

Jack Caldwell Jr. and
his wife Stephanie

Lisa Caldwell Welch and her
husband Randy
(Photo by Jenny Krummel)

Amy Caldwell Torres and her husband Phillip

After Cynthia passed away, I thought I could never fall in love again; however, two years later, I married Gin. We have known each other since my days in Crawfordsville. *(Photo by Vicki Bomke Thomson)*

Gin and I frequently return to Crawfordsville. In 2008, we enjoyed the town's fall festival with our former teacher Bobby Watson and his wife Mary Ann.

17.

Those difficult summer days prefaced a brighter chapter in my life. It would have been so easy to quit school, but I returned to Crawfordsville on the faith that I would find a place to live. With the luck of the Irish, I did. Essie Long, known to everyone as Aunt Essie, offered me an arrangement that we dubbed "three hots and a cot"; in other words, she provided me three hot meals and a place to sleep. She also laundered my clothes. Mrs. Long charged me just twelve dollars a week. I know that doesn't sound like much money today, but I didn't have much money to pay. A wrinkled little lady in her mid-sixties, Aunt Essie walked with a limp. It was obvious that she had lived a hard life. However, behind those horn-rimmed glasses was a champion of 42, which is a card game. Part of our agreement was that if her elderly group of friends needed a substitute for their weekly card game, I would step in. As a result, I became a very good 42 player and still am today.

Besides playing cards with senior citizens, my brain expanded in other areas. I became motivated to make good grades, thanks to my history teacher.

"Jackie, have your parents seen your report card?" Mr. Watson asked when I turned it in unsigned. Six weeks into the fall semester, that was one dilemma that I never saw coming. With Mama and Daddy residing in another state, how was that ever going to happen?

"No, sir," I answered nervously. "They moved to Texas."

"That so?" he asked. "Well, the school board requires the signature of an adult."

"Hmm … I never thought about it," I countered, keenly aware that my ears were growing warmer as the seconds ticked by. "What should I do?"

It was an unspoken fact that Bobby Watson had high standards and no patience with mediocrity. Tall and muscular, he looked every bit the part of his other title: Coach. In fact, Mr. Watson coached every sport that our school offered. Boys considered him a role model, while girls swooned over his chiseled features and curly brown hair. In life as well as in sports, Coach Watson believed that competition strengthened character for both sexes.

After a very long pause, Mr. Watson removed his reading glasses. "Tell you what," he suggested. I felt the tightness in my throat subside, as I breathed a long, dizzying sigh of relief. *Surely he's going to let me off the hook*, I thought. "Why don't I sign your report card?"

"Gee, thanks," I said. It wasn't exactly the solution I hoped for, and I wondered what I had gotten myself into. Now there was no slacking off, because Mr. Watson would be looking over my shoulder. It was definitely a good time to kick up my study habits.

Word traveled fast. It didn't take long for the teachers to share my plight among themselves. These educators and even their spouses took turns sharing their passion for knowledge. It was obvious that they all were anxious for me to succeed. It was a good thing, because I was hungry to learn.

History became my best subject, but it's hard to tell if that's because Mr. Watson was such a good teacher or because I loved learning about people and places of times gone by. In our little classroom, Mr. Watson had a way of making the past come to life so clearly that it felt as though I'd lived through the Battle of Gettysburg, taken a stroll in Red Square, or witnessed the construction of the Taj Mahal. In truth, I didn't know what was over the next mountain; the farthest I had ever traveled was Memphis. Hearing about what was going on in the rest of the world made me even more inquisitive and ready to soak up the culture of other states and countries. Chapters that we covered in Mr. Watson's class whet my appetite for travel. I longed to see and experience the rest of the planet in person.

Herman Philips, who taught shop and agriculture, presented the basics of crafts, such as woodworking and welding, as well as any activity that had to do with farming. Tall and thin with jet black hair, Mr. Philips was part American Indian. His interactive lessons included field trips that showcased the many facets of livestock, from raising the meat to packing the meat.

"Don't kick a cow chip," Mr. Philips once quipped, standing knee deep in the cornfield of a nearby farm. "That might be your next boss." I supposed it was true, but I didn't plan a career that included cow chips. Having sharecropped with my parents, I had no desire to farm for a living. By then, I knew that my expertise leaned toward the business side.

I was impressed that Mr. Philips was so patient, and it made me proud to overhear him tell another teacher that I was one of his best students, certainly not because I excelled at the crafts he taught, but simply because I listened. Unlike my classmates, free time could not be spent relaxing or doing anything that did not generate income. Once in class, I focused on staying awake and paying attention.

Like Mr. Watson, Mr. Philips demonstrated that learning did not stop at the end of the class day. This tall, thin Mississippi native covered so many subjects not directly related to the one he taught—how to balance a checkbook, ways to stretch a dollar, and the importance of courtesy in our daily dealings—but every bit as useful. He even took a group of us boys to his hometown of Gulfport to crab in the Gulf of Mexico.

Certainly, Mr. Watson and Mr. Philips were among the busiest people in town. In addition to coaching and teaching history, Mr. Watson drove a school bus. Mr. Philips was also a school bus driver and worked with the Future Farmers of America. Both educators had children of their own, but they generously gave their undivided attention to students whenever the need arose.

Of course, I can't forget my English teacher, Christine Riley. Frail and tiny, it was rumored that her red hair turned redder when she got mad. Although crippled by rheumatoid arthritis, she insisted that her husband deliver her to Crawfordsville High School every day. Mrs. Riley was so dedicated to teaching that she actually told me I flunked ninth grade English. Reluctantly, I repeated the subject as a sophomore. When the office checked close to graduation, my record revealed an excess credit in English.

"Hey, I found out that you didn't actually flunk me," I told her.

"I know I didn't, but you still needed to take it over," she said with a smile. In the process, I had grown to love literature and can still quote Shakespeare.

Then there was Bonnie Gresham, who taught chemistry. She insisted I retake a test after noticing my score was substantially higher than usual.

"Jackie, did you cheat on that test?" she demanded to know. I was no match for her domineering personality. Besides, she was married to our principal, who had already chastised me for shooting craps at school.

"No, I just referred to the notes you gave us in class," I said meekly.

"Well, that's cheating," she retorted. Her tightly permed gray hair bobbed with authority. "You can't use outside help."

Sure enough, my grade on the retake was a C, which was closer to my actual comprehension of the subject.

Looking back, I realize that I was not the only kid these teachers influenced. Many other youngsters were in the same boat, just trying to make a living and do their best. We were fortunate to have educators who never stopped preparing us for life in the real world. I didn't believe that college would be any different.

18.

Christmas in Crawfordsville was by far the most wonderful time of the year. It wasn't just the music in the air or the pungent fragrance of freshly cut cedar trees. It wasn't the festively decorated homes with their wreathed porches and colored lights that I remember so vividly. Without question, it was the spirit of generosity—alive and well in the hearts of Crawfordsville residents—that made the holiday so special. It was such a happy time. There was truly nowhere else on earth I'd rather be celebrating the season of Christ's birth.

When I lived at home, there were lean years when we didn't get an apple or orange for Christmas. After my family moved and I began to make my own way in the world, the true meaning of Christmas took on a deeper dimension. To my surprise, other people opened their pockets and shared their Christmases with me. Even those without much to give found a way to make things easier for others, including myself, who were struggling to survive. Miss Catherine and friends always gave me a nice piece of change, and I had a place for every nickel. Once I used these funds to buy a new jacket; another year I bought a pair of shoes. As poor as I was, I felt grateful to have a little money in the bank when there were others who did not. Somehow I think others knew, and maybe even saw the probability, that I would excel one day. It became my goal not to disappoint them.

The first Christmas season after my family moved to Texas produced a unique and scary holiday memory. Every day, as closing time drew near, it was my job to hose down the meat market, which contained the store's only working air conditioner. With its 220 volts of electricity, caution was paramount. Unfortunately, caution wasn't on my mind as I hosed the floor and reached to pull the electrical cord from my path. Suddenly a shock ran through my body. To my horror, sparks flew and crackled. I was unable to let go of the cord. Shaking uncontrollably, I struggled to holler for help, but any sounds I formed were hopelessly lodged deep in my throat. A sharp pain paralyzed me from the top of my head to the tip of my toes. Somewhere inside my body was a mind that still worked, but every morsel of physical strength had been zapped.

Thank goodness that God was once again looking over my shoulder and sent an angel to rescue me. Miss Jane, initially immersed in her end-of-day rituals, had witnessed the entire accident. In a flash that seemed like an eternity, she leaped from the other side of the room with strength that I didn't know she had. The quick-thinking Miss Jane slammed her stocky body into mine with an impact that knocked both of us to the floor, far away from the unit.

"Holy mackerel!" she wailed. "Jackie, are you okay?"

"What was that?" I asked, thrilled to find that my voice still worked. I was enormously grateful to be free of the electricity's spell and even more grateful to have no ill long-term effects from my terrifying encounter.

That year, Christmas Eve fell on a Saturday, the day of the week that Griffin Grocery stayed open until midnight. Business was brisk all day, as people rushed in and out to purchase last-minute food and supplies. Caught up in the frenzy, I hadn't had any time to think about missing my parents, brother, and sisters; however, I should have known that Miss Jane was thinking for both of us. Just before the stroke of midnight, she locked the doors and scurried to the back of the store. I could tell that she was up to something.

"Jackie," Miss Jane whispered, "how about you and me have us some Christmas cheer?" She poured each of us a glass of eggnog and we toasted the spirit of the season. I also celebrated the fact that my employer had saved my life.

19.

Working at Griffin Grocery was an education in itself. Not only did I learn the ins and outs of operating a retail business, but I was also exposed to all types of people and how they chose to spend their hard-earned paychecks. In truth, everyone was just trying to get by. Occasionally, my job also opened doors that led to extra income. Never again did I want to sleep with a brick for a pillow, so I was always on the prowl for new and innovative ways to increase my bank account. In at least one instance, my youthful ambition could have been my downfall.

Regular as clockwork, an elderly black gentleman came to the store every Saturday to buy three hundred pounds of chopped corn, a variety normally used to feed chickens or hogs. Tom, a widower, lived alone in a shotgun-style house, about three miles from town. With the Griffins' permission, I always drove him home. He was a small man and needed help unloading his large order.

Back then, there were tales of whiskey brewing deep in the woods that bordered Crawfordsville. Those who engaged in such a risky practice did so by cooking corn in a portable copper pipe distillery, carefully hidden in the middle of the woods. When used as designed, the still forced the temperature high enough to produce steam and emit a vapor that resulted in pure alcohol. It was common knowledge that if you walked up on a still cooking, it was best to just turn around and walk out. You didn't make any noise or "they" would shoot you. More than once, Jimmy Currie and I happened upon such an operation—sometimes two or three, and some more elaborate than others—while we were squirrel hunting. Each time, we managed to leave without incident. We were also cautioned to hunt only on the west side of the woods. I feared that Tom, who resided near the east side, was cooking a little chopped corn for some home brew. On this particular Saturday, after several weeks of making small talk, the suspense was more than I could stand.

"Tom, what are you doing with all that corn?" I blurted out shortly after parking at his house.

More flustered than irritated, Tom flashed a broad smile. "Why, that's chicken feed, Mr. Jackie," he said. "I got lots of chickens."

"Tom, I don't see no chickens," I said.

"Oh, they're out back," he insisted, climbing out of the truck. He waved his arms with a touch of drama. "I have a big hen house. and I keep them all in that hen house."

"Tom, are you telling me the truth?" I asked, unconvinced.

This time he winced, as if deep in thought. "Come on, I'll show you what's happening."

Trusting that Tom would confide in me, I jumped out of the truck and scurried to catch up. He was already making tracks down the gravel trail. After walking several hundred yards, we came to a clearing of sorts, and I realized that my hunch was right. Right in front of us, but not visible from the road, was indeed a still, bubbling away. Sure enough, Tom was cooking corn.

"Tom, how much would you charge me for a gallon of that corn whiskey?" I asked, intrigued by the process.

"For you, Mr. Jackie, three dollars," he answered with pride. His brown eyes glittered as he continued, "You can even cut this with water and make two gallons, and it will still be about eighty proof."

To my amazement, Tom continued to talk, and I became an eager listener. "Now I'm going to show you the difference between good corn liquor and bad," he said.

I watched with fascination as Tom poured some of the forbidden potion in an ashtray and struck a match. A bright blue flame ascended from the hot liquid. "That's the sign of real good corn liquor," he explained. "It's pure. If you ever see any that burns a red flame, don't drink that, 'cause it will kill you."

My ears perked up at his next suggestion. "Now, what you can do is get you some brown sugar and heat it slowly in a pan," Tom said. "Add just enough of it, and it will turn your corn whiskey to the most beautiful caramel color that looks just like bottled and bonded whiskey."

Tom's directions were clear. In fact, they were a little too clear. I was a fast learner. Within days, I was duplicating his recipe, even making two gallons out of one. Later, I'd cut the brew once again to produce three gallons from one. Now the mixture was not eighty proof; it was sixty proof. To package my product by the pint, I picked up empty wine bottles along the road, then washed and scalded them.

Before long, I was a successful entrepreneur with a steady customer base. School dances produced easy revenue. While my friends were rock 'n' rolling inside the community center, I was outside exchanging my special formula for real cash.

Fortunately, I came to my senses and quit selling corn liquor by my senior year. The last straw came when people started calling me on

Sundays. True, I was making corn liquor, but I certainly wasn't going to sell it on the Lord's day.

It turned out that while not everybody knew that I was making corn liquor, more folks knew than I thought did. Imagine my surprise forty-five years later, when the subject came up as Miss Catherine, my wife, Cynthia, and I were dining in Houston.

"Jackie, a drink of that good whiskey you used to sell would sure taste good right now," Miss Catherine said.

I almost choked on my steak. "Where are you coming from?" I croaked in disbelief.

"I know you sold some whiskey in high school."

"You don't know any such thing!"

"Yes, I do," she laughed. "I know when you got in and when you got out. If you hadn't gotten out, I would have jerked you out."

Thank goodness angels were watching out for me in Crawfordsville. Miss Catherine knew when to stay quiet and when to sound off. She gave me just enough freedom to do the right thing. During the few months that my enterprise flourished, not one buyer went blind or became sick. I am thankful that I never got caught, and no one made a big deal of it. At any rate, my brief business venture helped to keep gas in the truck that Daddy left behind.

20.

Writing to Mama helped to fill the void of not being around her every day. So many times I missed hearing her advice or just sharing the news of my day. Even trivial events seem more important when relayed to someone who has known you all your life. Several months earlier, I wrote Mama a letter, and not having any paper to my name, carefully scribbled some words on a square of toilet paper.

As the weather turned colder, my heart grew heavier. Two holiday seasons had come and gone since my family had left Arkansas for the Texas Gulf Coast. Christmas was almost here, and I missed my family more than ever. Don't misunderstand; the folks in Crawfordsville were generous and kindhearted. They were always including me in their festivities. But that year, I longed to see my kin.

I had a gut feeling that Miss Catherine sensed my depression. Not wanting to spoil her holiday cheer, I tried to look happy when I arrived for our weekly Sunday visit. Her home was decked out in style for the holidays, and I could tell that she was ready to celebrate.

"Come on in out of the cold," she motioned, opening the door before I even grazed the doorbell. "I have a surprise for you." That afternoon Miss Catherine glowed even more than usual. From behind her back, she whipped out a long, brown envelope and handed it to me. "Go ahead and open it," she urged, fully immersed in the suspense of the moment. "It's an early Christmas present."

Bewildered, I tore open the flap and blinked in disbelief. Inside was a bus ticket to Houston that bore my name. It was as though Miss Catherine had read my mind. How could she know that nothing would please me more? I was already counting the hours and minutes until the bus departed. The prospect of seeing my family and visiting the great state of Texas was the best gift ever.

Finally the time came for me to visit my family. Never mind that it was my first time on a regular commercial bus. Excitement turned to anticipation as I shivered in the darkness at the appointed stop in West Memphis, where Miss Jane had driven me. All I could think about was that at the end of this six-hundred-mile ride, Mama, Daddy, and my little sisters would be waiting. I was especially eager to see the transformation that Texas had made in my parents' lives. Everything, I was told, was bigger and better in the Lone Star State.

There was no turning back when the dusty silver Continental Trailways bus lumbered into the station and heaved to a halt. I took final inventory of my belongings: a canvas suitcase borrowed from Miss Catherine, three one-dollar bills, and a care package with some food to eat along the way, and climbed the steps. There was barely time to present my ticket to the driver when the vehicle unexpectedly lurched forward. Thrown sideways, I landed in the nearest available seat and made myself at home next to a window. The other passengers, who were snoring, chattering, or snacking, seemed comfortably settled into their surroundings, but the experience was all still new to me. I tightly clasped the bundle so lovingly prepared by Miss Catherine and Miss

Jane, and considered consuming its contents. Not yet, I decided, too excited to eat or drink.

Every few miles, the bus stopped briefly to pick up more riders along the way. Sometimes we were prompted to change buses. I managed to stay on course, transferring vehicles only three or four times. I wanted to catch a glimpse of the passing countryside, but in the foggy darkness, only my reflection was visible in the smudged glass. Exhausted, I finally surrendered to the bouncing cadence of the bus. Gradually I began to drift in and out of consciousness. When I awoke, dawn was breaking, and the welcome warmth of day was streaming through the windows.

"Are we in Texas?" I asked the old gentleman next to me.

"Almost," he answered. He scratched his beard and stared at my lap.

I had forgotten about the package of food. I gobbled up the sandwich, potato chips, and apple, leaving only a roll of Lifesavers behind. Even the almost-empty paper bag smelled like the special angels who had prepared it. Until that morning, I had never cared much for Lifesavers and opted to stash the wintergreen candy in my pocket. Maybe, I thought, I'll give it to little Carolyn as a surprise.

I dozed off again. It must have been hours later that I glanced around and noticed that many of the original travelers were no longer on the bus. By now, I was feeling like an old hand at bus travel, savoring a seniority of sorts, at least until my growling stomach interrupted. It was almost noon, hours since I had downed the goodies in my care package. I reconsidered the Lifesavers tucked safely inside my pocket. Once I pulled the waxy string, eating just one was nearly impossible. Soon the entire roll disappeared, and in the process, wintergreen Lifesavers became my favorite candy.

A gigantic Welcome to Texas sign boldly marked the state line. I passed the time by soaking in the sights and sounds as the miles rolled by, thinking of how people and events had impacted my life, and imagining what was to come. By early evening, I could only hope that this marathon on wheels was almost over. Several more hours passed, and I nodded off one last time, determined to wake up when the driver announced my destination. Instead, I was stirred by the buzz of passengers, commenting about lights in the distance. Sure enough, there were more buildings ahead of us than I had seen in my entire life. Twenty-four hours after leaving Crawfordsville, it was a relief to arrive at the bus station in Houston.

There was no one waiting for me in the middle of the night, probably because Mama and Daddy didn't know what time to expect me. I was beckoned to the terminal restaurant by the smell of sizzling beef patties.

"How much are your hamburgers?" I asked the waitress, a large, homely woman with bleached blond hair.

"Forty-five cents," she said. "Do you want one?"

"Sure," I answered. "How about a Coke and potato chips?"

"Everything's under a dollar," she explained. No words could be sweeter. I was elated to have solid food so reasonably priced within my budget.

Ten minutes later, the waitress delivered what appeared to be a huge hamburger. Even though it was served with a Coke and chips, I was convinced that this combo belonged to another customer. Being careful not to touch the food, I waited for the waitress to reappear. She glanced in my direction but was in no hurry to respond.

"Hey, I didn't order this," I finally called out.

"You ordered a hamburger, didn't you?" she answered. It was clear that I was testing her patience.

"Yes, but this is bigger than what I ordered," I insisted.

"Son, where are you from?"

"Arkansas."

"Well, that's your hamburger. Everything is bigger in Texas!"

Without delay, I wolfed down the entire meal.

Although I was thrilled to see my parents, the visit came with mixed emotions. There were still some hard feelings between my siblings and me, because I had opted to stay in Arkansas instead of moving to Texas.

In addition, Daddy's behavior was even more offensive. His problems were compounded by jealousy. He went so far as to resent the time that Mama spent with me. Once in a violent outburst, he tried his best to whup her. I didn't hesitate to intervene.

"If I ever see you hit Mama again, I'm going to give you some of that happiness," I promised. As far as I know, my father never tried to harm her again. After that, I suspected he hated me, because I took away his punching bag.

It didn't take long for me to miss my life in Crawfordsville. Several weeks later, I hitched a ride home.

21.

Between my junior and senior years in high school, I signed on to work as a deck hand. Our barge traveled the Intercoastal Canal, a route that allowed me to once again visit with my family in LaPorte, Texas. This time, Patsy, who had been attending church services, announced that she had someone special for me to meet. It was her friend, Cynthia. I figured that if the two knew each other from church, I could trust Patsy's judgment. I had no way of knowing that the introduction would change my life.

The day after we docked, my sister and I arrived at Cynthia's house. Patsy was feeling smug in her role as matchmaker; I was feeling a little nervous because I agreed to this arrangement. Knock, knock, knock, and a little cutie with short, dark hair and green eyes opened the door to greet us. *Wow*, I thought. *Patsy has good taste!*

Cynthia ushered us inside, and it didn't take long for me to see why my sister held her friend in such high regard. I was spellbound by this beautiful fifteen-year-old with an upbeat personality. I found Cynthia to be a good listener and a lot of fun to talk with. I learned that her mother had passed away several years earlier, and she lived with her father, Arthur Faulkenberry, a pilot in World War II, who worked for Humble Oil.

"If you've got the time, we'll have lunch or something tomorrow, without Patsy," I found myself saying as we left.

It took forever for today to become tomorrow. Finally it was time for the date. It was going pretty well, I thought, while downing a hamburger combo with Cynthia at The Corral, a popular drive-in restaurant in downtown LaPorte.

"What would you like to do now?" I inquired, finishing the last French fry.

"Would you like to see where I grew up?" Cynthia asked. "We can go to Tri City Beach. It's only about thirteen miles from here."

Her suggestion sounded perfect to me. We were cruising along and having no trouble making conversation when my rear-view mirror reflected an unwelcome visitor. Flashing lights, punctuated by the blast of a siren, announced my indiscretion. I pulled over and prepared to be chastised.

A hefty policeman climbed out of the squad car and walked to the window. "Son, do you know how fast you were going?" he asked gruffly.

"No, sir," I answered in my most polite voice. "I guess we were busy talking."

Instinctively, I handed over my driver's license, and he walked behind the car to record the vehicle identification. Being pulled over is one thing, but being apprehended in front of Cynthia on our very first date was more than a little embarrassing.

"Well, this should help you remember," he said, scribbling a ticket without looking up. Almost jubilantly, he ripped the citation from his pad and handed it to me.

"How much will this cost?" I asked, hoping that this officer of the law would reconsider. "I'm just visiting and want to clear it right away."

Maybe he'll feel sorry for me since I don't live here, I thought. *Maybe he'll even tear it up and let me drive off with Cynthia.*

"Ten or fifteen dollars," he said, matter-of-factly. "You can pay it at the station in town. Drive safely."

He drove off to catch other offenders. The episode left me red faced, but I was relieved when Cynthia's sympathetic look dissolved into a giggle. So much for first impressions, I thought, before heading off to settle my debt.

I was not about to give up on Tri City Beach. Once the ticket was paid, we continued on our course. Along the way, Cynthia confided that she never really cared for the beach, even though it was home at one time.

"There's hardly ever anyone here," she said. "It's too far away from town to have any neighbors." I nodded in agreement, knowing all too well what loneliness felt like. It was hard to imagine someone with such a talent for conversation being content in near isolation. Already, I sensed that we had much in common.

I pulled off the road next to an old cemetery and heard the sweet crunch of oyster shells beneath the wheels as the motor ground to a halt. At long last, we could talk without interruption. I turned toward Cynthia and placed my right arm on top of the seat behind her head. Now it was just the two of us, surrounded by the sun, sky, and a soothing sea breeze.

To my dismay, Cynthia squinted, as if something familiar had just caught her attention.

"My mother is buried right over there," she said.

"You're kidding," I quipped, but her reaction told me she was not.

"Get out, and I'll show you." Although I didn't know her mother, I definitely felt a presence. It was at least enough to break the mood. I could only hope for other dates.

22.

Paul and I often took Jimmy hunting and fishing, and sometimes we doubled on dates. Although Jimmy never complained, it was evident that he wasn't having as much fun as the two of us were. He didn't want sympathy, but it was difficult to see a person like him go through what he did. I would have done anything, and sometimes did, to bring back the life he had lost.

By my senior year in high school, Paul had joined the Army, and Jimmy was living at his parents' farm. Although physically impaired, Jimmy no longer had the stress of studying for classes. That December, when his parents were out of town, he surprised me with an invitation to go duck hunting. The very fact that my good friend was feeling restless and ready for entertainment was a good sign. Truth be known, I didn't have the heart to refuse him. Unfortunately, I felt terrible and was absolutely certain that I had a bad case of the flu.

"I don't think I can go," I sputtered. "I'm too sick."

"Aw, come on," he pleaded. "I'll bundle you up, and you'll be fine. It'll be fun."

There was no reasoning with Jimmy, who had a knack for convincing even the most stubborn person to see things his way. Don't ask me why I did.

I spent the night before our outing at Jimmy's house, so we could get an early start. Believe it or not, it was a school night. When Jimmy woke me at 3 the next morning, I had second thoughts. My head pounded, and my throat was even scratchier than the previous afternoon. Thankfully, any reluctance banished when I saw his face. After all that Jimmy had been through physically and mentally, it was good to see him enjoying life and regaining a sense of normalcy.

In the pitch darkness, we headed about eight miles to Miller Cypress Lake, towing Jimmy's old johnboat behind us. Had we not fished and hunted the area dozens of times before, our expedition would have been even more dangerous to navigate. Where was the moon when we needed it? As we approached the lake, our favorite spot was encased by a thick fog and appeared oddly sinister. Jimmy wasted no time in shining the lantern so I could unhitch the boat.

"Yikes, it's freezing out here," I said, brushing my hand against the vessel's aluminum side. "You sure you want to do this?"

"Hurry up!" he chided. "The ducks will be here soon."

The temperature had to be below freezing as I lifted Jimmy on board. Slowly and deliberately, we drifted into the water, leaving the muddy bank behind us. The raucous grind of the motor sounded almost irreverent in the quiet darkness of the early morning.

Now I really felt miserable. We could only see a couple of feet in front of us, and I feared what might be lurking farther ahead and beneath us. Who would report me missing if I failed to make it to class on time? Feeling sick to my stomach erased any desire to hunt. I thought I was going to die. Drowsy with fever, I sunk deeper into my jacket and adjusted the collar to shield the biting cold from my numb ears. A hard jolt shook the boat.

"What was that?" I yelped.

"We've hit ice," Jimmy said. "Boat won't go any farther. Guess we'll have to shoot from here."

Great, I thought, figuring that it was around 4:30 by then. Surely the ducks would be flying overhead soon. With the temperature in the teens, even minutes seemed like hours.

As daylight crept closer, the welcome medley of flapping wings and hasty honks broke the eerie silence. Mallards! Primed for such a moment, Jimmy aimed and fired his rifle. A distinctive plop, repeated seconds apart, confirmed our hopes. About forty yards away lay four dead greenheads, esteemed trophies in the world of duck hunting. We gunned the motor to retrieve the birds, but once again, after going only half the distance, we hit ice. Obviously, Jimmy's fallen fowl were not within our reach. My friend's monumental kill meant nothing to me, except that our expedition was over, and we could finally go home. I was ready to enjoy a toasty ride back to civilization.

"Let's go," I said.

"Not yet!" Jimmy snapped. "I've gotta get the ducks."

"Look," I said. "There's no way to reach them. The boat can't cross the water, and if we get out, we're bound to fall through the ice." I struggled to start the boat, now surrounded by ice. It wasn't budging. After several failed attempts, I doubled a fist and smacked the ice so hard that it bruised my knuckles. As the surface broke, I turned to share the good news with Jimmy.

"Hey," I gasped. To my horror, Jimmy was in the lake, inching his limp body toward the ducks. "Are you crazy?"

Without thinking, I tore off my boots and jumped into the frigid, chest-high water. Within seconds, I hoisted Jimmy and his prized bundle of lifeless birds into the boat. Somehow we managed to make it to dry land, gather our wits, and head back to town shortly after dawn.

Naturally Jimmy insisted that we stop along the way and show the ducks to anyone who remotely cared. Feeling deathly sick, I was more concerned about getting to school on time. My goal was to graduate, and nothing, not even pneumonia, was going to stop me.

That afternoon, I parted with five dollars at the office of Dr. Hare. It was lucky for me that Crawfordsville's only physician had the gold standard of drugs—penicillin, administered through a syringe that he yanked from the floral wallpaper of his examining room.

23.

By April of 1958, graduation was all that my classmates could talk about. I looked forward to the event itself, which was only a month away, but I lacked the same anticipation as my friends whose families had supported them throughout their journeys. Even so, I wasn't depressed. I knew that my special angels, Miss Jane and Miss Catherine, would be there. I had no plans to order graduation invitations, but Miss Jane was one step ahead of me.

"Jackie, you got some relatives?" she asked. As was often the case, I had not eaten all day and was consuming a bologna, tomato, and onion sandwich at work.

"Yes," I replied, intercepting her thoughts, "but I don't want to send anything to them. Besides, I don't think I've done anything more special than millions of other kids."

"Now, don't say that," she said. "You really should send out invitations. Look how far you've come and what you've accomplished. You've made a lot of sacrifices to walk across that stage. I know they are proud of you. After all, it's not every day that a person graduates from high school. It's a milestone for them, too."

Reluctantly, I ordered a box of invitations, and together, Miss Jane and I compiled a list of recipients. Within days after the envelopes were mailed, it was like Christmas. A variety of gifts began to arrive: a shirt, some cash, a pen set, a pair of pants, a wallet, and other things that I needed for college, with hearty wishes from all of my friends. Not one relative sent even a note of congratulations. Following the etiquette she so strongly practiced, Miss Jane even wrote my thank-you notes.

Perhaps, I reasoned, my family is going to bring their presents to the ceremony. I didn't care about receiving anything except my diploma. It would be enough of a surprise just to have some kin show up.

At long last, the momentous day arrived. My hopes and spirits were high as I dressed in a royal blue and white cap and gown to walk across the auditorium stage with my ten classmates. (I later found out that four received blank envelopes because their graduation requirements had not been met.) When my name was called, I looked straight ahead, shook our principal's hand, and accepted my diploma. Applause, followed by cheers, erupted from the audience.

I paused at the corner of the stage and scanned the sea of Crawfordsville citizens, a crowd pleased to be celebrating the bright promise of its youth. Some individuals, I noticed, did not even have a relative in our class. My eyes searched for any sign of family—my parents, sisters, brother, an aunt, uncle, or cousin—but it was no use. The ovation came courtesy of my friends, led by Miss Catherine and Miss Jane. That day, I realized that these two angels, beaming from the front row, and many who reveled in the occasion—teachers, customers, co-workers, and other parents—had also become my family.

Although Miss Catherine tried her best to convince me to go to Memphis State, I chose a college a bit farther away but it was at least in the same state. Even though she generously helped me to cover costs,

I was determined to avoid the pricey out-of-state tuition. Penny-wise and dollar-smart, my new school was scarcely an hour's drive from home; however, it was worlds apart in so many ways. The freshman class numbered nine hundred, only one-third more inhabitants than the entire town of Crawfordsville.

Having visited Arkansas State in Jonesboro for Future Farmers of America milk and cattle-judging competitions, I assumed that finding my way around as a student would be easy. Not so. No doubt my freshman English professor possessed either a sense of humor or a strange curiosity when he chose that very topic as a writing assignment. Needless to say, I had no trouble penning, "My first day at Arkansas State, I was as confused as a sterile rabbit."

Once again, a grocery store—this time, Big Star—provided gainful employment. I earned a dollar an hour, but there were not many places to work in a college town, and at least a hundred kids waited to take my place.

To save money, I convinced the college's business administrator to subtract the required amount for "board" from the "room and board." As a checker during store hours and a stocker after hours, I was not on the same dining schedule as other students. I became adept at squeezing my food budget to the limit by abstaining from breakfast. A dime bought lunch, usually a pack of cheese crackers and soda water. A quarter was enough for a can of tomato soup, a sleeve of saltine crackers, and a soft drink, which served as dinner on most nights. Occasionally, I splurged on a jar of pickled pigs feet.

Because I had never lived in more than a cubby hole, adapting to dorm life was easy. My roommate, a fellow with thick glasses and high-water pants, was rarely in the room, and he seemed more interested in making stink bombs to implode on the floor above us than actually cracking the books. My guess was that he wouldn't last long.

My suitemate, Jerry Tucker, and I became good friends. Like me, Jerry hailed from a rural part of the state where his parents owned a small grocery store. He was a math major, and to me, he was the smartest kid on campus. He was as close to a genius as anyone I had ever known.

24.

Meanwhile, Cynthia and I maintained a long-distance courtship. In June of 1960, I was once again working on the barge and was in the process of making a tow from Port Arthur to New Orleans. My hands stayed busy, but my head was stuck in the clouds, daydreaming about Cynthia and our magical evening at her junior-senior prom. Dressed in a white lace evening gown, no bride could have been more beautiful. Before I left Texas, I asked her to be my wife.

"I'm so tired of being alone," I began. "What are the chances of us getting married?"

"Daddy will never allow it," she said. "Not until I finish school."

I didn't argue. I knew the value of education and had to agree that her father was right.

Employment on a barge was far from dull. Our crew included a captain, a pilot, two engine room technicians, and two deckhands. Deckhands also served as cooks, and we worked six hours on, six hours off. Weathering terrible storms was part of the adventure. In the midst of one particularly bad storm, I had to cut all the barges loose in order to keep our vessel afloat. After the storm, we rounded up and fastened all the barges to our boat and took off again. Once I even fell overboard but was fortunate to be spotted and rescued by another crew member. Barge work could be perilous, but I didn't have the sense to be scared. I savored those experiences not normally available to the average person.

My job was educational as well as financially rewarding. Because I lived on the boat, I was able to save every penny of my salary. In our spare time, six of us played poker for real money, and Lady Luck often smiled my way. Some of the guys asked for loans to tide them over until payday, but I was saving to buy a car when I returned to Memphis.

"Hey, Jackie, you have a call," I heard someone shout in the midst of a poker game. My ordinary day was about to become extraordinary.

My heart skipped a beat. No one had ever phoned me on the boat, and I worried that Mama or Miss Catherine had fallen ill or been in an accident. Expecting the worst, I grabbed the receiver.

"Come and get me," a familiar feminine voice said.

I could hardly believe my ears. Now my heart really skipped a beat. "Cynthia! You want to get married?" I asked, praying that this was not a joke.

"Just come and get me," she said.

"As soon as we dock, I'm driving to pick you up," I promised. All the letter writing and loneliness were about to end.

When the barge docked, I purchased a canary yellow 1955 Buick Special. My anticipation in driving to the Lone Star State to make Cynthia my bride produced almost more excitement than I could fathom.

Another phone call disturbed my frenzied packing. "Jackie," Cynthia said solemnly, "Daddy wants to talk with you."

"Listen here," a deep voice boomed. I visualized my future father-in-law's partially bald head turning red. "You and my daughter are not getting married, and I don't ever want you to come to our house again!"

Stunned, but empowered by the challenge, I thought, am I going to let those words scare me away? This was another major decision I was going to make in my life. I continued packing as if our conversation had never occurred.

Cynthia and I knew that we weren't old enough to legally wed. In the state of Texas, eighteen was the minimum age for a woman to marry, and it was twenty-one for a man. With each of us one year shy of the requirements, we needed our parents' consent to apply for the marriage license. I felt sure that Mama would sign for me, but convincing Cynthia's father to sign for her would be my finest feat yet.

The next day, I drove to Eureka Springs, Arkansas, where Mama and Daddy were working. Mama was happy to accompany me back to Texas, and, once again, it was just the two of us. I enjoyed sharing this one-on-one journey as we reminisced about old and harder times along the way. Each turn of the tires reinforced my resolve, bringing me closer to Cynthia and our new life together. In a strange way, I looked forward to the confrontation that was about to happen.

"I'm going to ask you, but if you don't agree with me, we're going to get married anyway," I said hurriedly, as Mr. Faulkenberry opened the door. He glanced over my shoulder and spotted Mama, smiling sweetly in the front seat. After some heated words, he reluctantly gave in.

With Cynthia's father and my mother poised to sign the all-important document, there appeared to be a slight glitch. We discovered that Mama's identification was in the purse that she accidentally left at a roadside park in Arkansas. After some time, the court allowed her to sign an affidavit stating that she was my mother.

Never mind the details. Nothing could upset me on July 21, 1960, the happiest day of my life. There were no candles, flowers, or organ music as Cynthia and I breathlessly waited to say the vows that would make us husband and wife. We found ourselves side by side in the judge's chambers of the Harris County Municipal Courthouse in downtown Houston.

I know that the words we heard and the promises we exchanged had been repeated thousands of times before at that same location. To us, their cadence rang fresh and new. Dizzy with joy, every phrase spoken, "for richer or poorer, in sickness and in health ..." validated our love and hope for the future. Sealed with a kiss, we were finally pronounced man and wife.

I gazed at Cynthia and felt incredibly lucky to be married to the love of my life. They say that any good picnic ground is worth walking through several briar patches. After all the trials, tribulations, and hardships that I had endured, the good Lord finally sent me something good—a lovely girl to be my soul mate. Cynthia was worth any time, energy, and test of faith that I had endured along the way. Things were definitely starting to look up.

With the ceremony over, I asked the justice of the peace what he charged to conduct our ceremony. "Whatever you think she's worth," he said, nodding in Cynthia's direction. My near-empty wallet contradicted the fact that my new bride was priceless. The good judge looked amused when I handed over five dollars. "Look out the window," he said, pointing to a building across the street. "That's where you get a divorce if it doesn't work out."

There was no flying rice to dodge as we exited the air-conditioned courthouse and entered the southeast Texas humidity, amplified by the concrete and steel that surrounded us. A photographer wasn't around to officially record the momentous occasion, but we never needed a snapshot to spur the memory of our perfect day.

Unlike on most honeymoon departures, a parent—my dear mother—was in the back seat. Although Mama had done us a favor by signing the necessary papers, driving her back to Arkansas would be a very long trip.

25.

Cynthia's father may have signed the papers for her to marry me, but he had a hard time accepting another man in his daughter's life. Clearly used to being in charge, Arthur Faulkenberry made it his business to tell me what to do and what not to do. One day, he crossed the line and caught me sick and tired of his meddling.

"If you ever lay a hand on my daughter, you'll have me to answer to," he told me, with teeth clenched beneath his grey moustache.

Insulted by the very suggestion, I drew a deep breath and prepared to say what needed saying. "Look, I respect your daughter, and I respect you," I answered. "Now, she's my wife, and you don't ever tell me what to do as long as you live."

Cynthia was horrified by my response, but I had no regrets. To our mutual amazement, his demeanor eventually softened, and he began to back off.

My own personality also started to improve. After leaving home, I had become callous to the point that some people accused me of having ice water in my veins. It's not that I meant to ignore others; it's simply that I was scraping for everything I could to make a living. Cynthia's influence was the catalyst that made the difference. She gently reminded me to be more patient and caring and to take time for others. With my bride by my side, my entire outlook was transformed.

One important decision that I made right after our wedding was that college could wait. Cynthia and I chose to settle in Texas, near Baytown, where I found work at Abe's Supermarket. For sure, the grocery business was the business I knew best.

We also rented a small frame house in LaPorte that was larger than my previous residences, but it didn't take us long to outgrow our space. Within a few months, we found another reason to celebrate. Our first child was due in August.

Cynthia's doctor wanted $125 before our baby was delivered. We had no health insurance, yet we managed to squeeze every penny in order to pay on schedule. As the weeks zipped by, Cynthia grew bigger and bigger, and our anticipation also grew.

My father-in-law, by now a good friend, called me at work with the impending news on August 21, 1961. "Cynthia's gone to the hospital," he frantically announced. "She's going to have the baby."

"How soon?" I asked, knowing there was not a way in the world that I could leave the store until late afternoon. It was an unusually busy day, and there was no one to take my place.

"I don't know," he said. "I'll call you back." For hours, I received steady updates, each one tempered with greater urgency.

I couldn't think of anything else but Cynthia, and I hoped that she was not in too much pain. I wanted so badly to be at her side, especially in time for the baby's arrival. "Please, God," I prayed. "Let me make it in time."

The memory of those trying hours blurred as I held little Jack for the first time. We were so thrilled and proud to be parents, and I thanked the Lord for answering my prayers. Looking at my newborn son and his beautiful mother, I felt no man could be more blessed.

Physically Jack resembled Cynthia's father. Being new parents was an adjustment for Cynthia and me, but with trial and error, we learned what to do. Thanks to colic, there were times when I swore that Houston built the 610 Loop, now a major freeway, just so I could drive Jack around to quiet his cries.

Now that "we" were "three," it was high time to make another dream come true. From an early age, one of my burning ambitions had always been to buy a house. Never in my life had my family owned a home. As sharecroppers, my parents were provided a tiny shack, but even that structure wasn't their own. Cynthia and I soon grew tired of paying rent and needed the extra room.

After a bit of shopping, we set our sights on a starter home in Pasadena. Although it needed repair, we saw possibilities in the 1,200-square-foot brick house with its three bedrooms, one bath, and single-car garage. The monthly payment of seventy-eight dollars stretched our air-tight budget, but no palace could please us more. We were overjoyed to move into our dream home at 1406 Marguerite Drive.

I remember those early days with great fondness. Snug inside our own four walls, Cynthia and I were as happy as clams. While I was at work, Cynthia cared for Jack and wasted no time in transforming our fixer-upper into a dollhouse. Settling in, my young wife itched to change the carpet, soiled and dingy from a dozen years of previous ownership. Of course, we had no money for new carpet, but Cynthia was not discouraged. In desperation, she peeked underneath.

"Ugh," she said. "Just take a look at this."

To my delight, her prying led to a wonderful surprise.

"Look what they covered up, hon," I said, giving the seam a strong tug. "We're going to use these nice hardwood floors."

"Are you sure?" she asked. "Look at the condition they're in. They're pretty worn out."

"The houses I lived in growing up had wood floors," I explained. "With a little work, we can make these shine."

Always game for a challenge, Cynthia worked around little Jack's schedule to restore the dull grain to its original luster. Her quest became a labor of love. Once finished, we agreed that even brand-new carpet could not have been a better decision.

With the floors refinished, Cynthia embarked on the outside landscaping. Handy with a hatchet, she fearlessly carved out every weed in her path, sometimes beheading a snake or two along the way. My energetic wife plotted and planted shrubs and flowers until our lawn was the showplace of the neighborhood. She loved gardening as much as Miss Catherine did. In fact, it was both comfort and coincidence that Cynthia possessed many of the same qualities as another angel in my life.

26.

Ironically, my induction into the corporate world began shortly after I dropped out of college to get married. About the time that Cynthia and I moved to Pasadena, my father-in-law encouraged me to interview with Humble Oil Company (now known as ExxonMobil) for a job opening in the refinery lab. Even though his suggestion sounded promising, I didn't jump at the opportunity. In reality, I knew nothing about refineries and had no idea what duties the position entailed. Naturally, I certainly didn't want Cynthia's dad held responsible for my performance. Having been on my own for so long, independence had become part of my nature. I shuddered at the scenario; it was a recipe for disaster.

Fate stepped in during a visit with one of our new neighbors, Joe Erhart. "Jackie, you ever thought about getting into sales?" he asked. "There's an opening in our company, and I think you'd be good for the job. We have a sales meeting next week, and you can come down and meet the powers that be."

My hopes sank as he described the attributes of the ideal candidate:

a minimum age of twenty-five years, a college degree, past military service, or ten years of sales experience.

"That disqualifies me right there," I said. "I'm only twenty, and I don't meet the other qualifications."

My neighbor was not deterred. "We'll fake it through," he said. "Besides, you look older than you are."

The next Monday, I drove to an office building off Allen Parkway, the gateway to downtown Houston. On the way, I thought about the prospect. Other than my grocery store and door-to-door experience, I had no sales background. Even so, I sat through the meeting and listened intently, hoping to get an idea of what might be in store. It was all Greek to me. Those in charge talked for a long time and thanked me for coming. They did not offer a job right away.

That evening, Joe met me in the yard. "Well, what did you think about it?" he inquired.

"Seems like y'all got it together," I replied, not quite knowing what to say.

"Think you'd like to be a part of it?" he continued.

"I don't know," I said, trying to buy a little time.

The next day, management called me back for a second interview and concluded our meeting by asking the same question.

"I'll tell you what," I said, concealing my enthusiasm. "That sounds fair enough, but I'd like to discuss this with my wife before I give you an answer."

"We expect you to," he replied. "If you want to bring her down here for a visit, we'll answer any questions."

All the way home, I mulled over the possibilities. The job offer consisted of a generous salary, a fast new Ford, an expense account, paid vacation, and an incentive program. Having a second car would mean that Cynthia and I didn't have to share transportation. The money would definitely come in handy. There would be a learning curve, but I had always loved a challenge. Being in a field with unlimited potential was certainly appealing.

By the time I arrived home, there was no question in my mind. "Hon, I'm not going to work for Humble," I announced. "I'm going to be a salesman."

The next Monday I launched my career with Lehn & Fink, selling household items to retail establishments. Houston was growing by leaps and bounds, and I could not have asked for a better territory. I thoroughly enjoyed my new job and soon realized that in one form or fashion, I had been selling almost my entire life. My previous jobs—from pedaling melons and eggs to minding the store at Griffin Grocery—served me well for the workload I faced. Each day, the learning curve grew a bit flatter.

The corporate world was all new to me. All I had ever known was to work hard and do well at what I did; however, there was more to this job than I had envisioned. Lehn & Fink furnished a good education in sales, but I also learned from my customers. I figured that if I were going to fish, I had to go where the fish swam. About 20 percent of the stores produced 80 percent of the business, so I began at one of the largest stores in Houston, called Sacco's, on the city's southwest side. It was a hectic day when I called on the manager. After waiting for what seemed forever, he finally agreed to see me. I could tell from his heavy-set frame that he enjoyed the grocery business. I could also tell that my timing was not good.

"Jackie, come into my office and sit down," Joe Chivoni said. "This is your first call, right?"

"Right," I said.

"Well, we're going to talk some generalities," he declared. "Let me tell you the dos and don'ts about this business. First, you've broken every rule there is. You show up without an appointment, then come in here when I'm busy and don't have the time to talk."

My ears stung, but I knew my new client was right. *Forget about getting an order from this guy,* I thought. *I've really blown it.* "But you're not going away without seeing me, so I think I should give you some words of advice," he continued. "After all, I feel sorry for you."

I squelched the urge to defend my actions and listened with interest while the manager took the time to explain what I should and should not do and how I should handle myself. Just when I felt certain that he was going to show me the door, Joe Chivoni gave me a huge order. I'll always be grateful for that first order, but I was especially grateful for his words of wisdom!

I made it a habit to start work early and stay late. Every minute counted. Aside from the financial benefits, I made many good friends in the grocery business, including Joe Chivoni.

Of course, it helped that I had quality merchandise to sell. Lysol spray was among the first products that I introduced to the Houston area, followed by a variety of fine Luden products as well as Elmer's, Andies, and Starlight mints. These products were referred to as change-makers in the industry. I also sold an assortment of candy bars, such as Payday, Butternut, Tootsie Rolls, Almond Joy, and Mounds. Before long, I was promoted to call on direct buy accounts, which included Kroger and the locally owned Weingarten's.

Unfortunately, several people at the company had been there a long time and were not quite as aggressive as I was. My sales were going straight up, while their sales were staying the same. Lehn & Fink was a good-old-boy club and my associates just wanted to keep their jobs, whether they were doing well or not. Good enough was definitely not what I wanted. It wouldn't have made any difference what job I undertook. Even if I were digging a ditch, I wanted to dig the best ditch. I took my job seriously, but my co-workers were personally offended that I outsold them. I refused to slack off just because others didn't like my work ethic. I knew that eventually rewards would come my way.

27.

The 1960s were successful on the home front as well. Cynthia and I welcomed three more children. Robert, who favored me in appearance, was born in 1962, before I even finished registering Cynthia at the hospital. When Lisa, our little red-haired daughter, was born in 1965, our family was ready for a bigger residence. We moved to Spring Branch, a rapidly growing suburb of west Houston, in 1968. Amy, who most closely resembled Cynthia, was born the following year.

Meanwhile, Mama and Daddy were almost as miserable as Cynthia and I were happy. I'd always known that if opposites attracted, my parents certainly qualified.

In many ways, Mama reminded me of a cat. A cat can be a sweet and lovable creature, but it screams if you step on its tail. My mother was the most loving person on earth, but she had no patience with my dad's womanizing ways. She loved Daddy to death, but as the old saying goes: "You always hurt the one you love." If things were not going right, her big blue eyes got even bigger, and she got mean. Mama played for keeps, not for fun.

Since I was old enough to understand, I tried to figure out what my dad was all about. Although he was a strong disciplinarian, Daddy didn't necessarily practice what he preached. He was a strict person with two distinct personalities, a drinking one and a sober one. When my father did not drink, he was a fine individual. When Daddy drank, he put liquor before his other obligations—an action I never understood. As a boy, I longed for my father to spend time with me, hunting and fishing. For whatever reason, it did not happen. Sadly, the two of us were never close, because his priorities were mixed up.

In contrast, Mama always made time for me, declaring more than once that she gave birth to five great children and one exceptional one. As the exceptional one, I now know why she loved me so much. From a very young age, I pined to see her smile, and it became my mission in life to give her a reason. In dirt-poor conditions, I didn't have the luxury of waiting until adulthood to help make ends meet. Always, I searched for ways to support my family. Without a doubt, Mama appreciated the little things—like making a fire in the stove when it was freezing—that I did to help her. Being resourceful was necessary for survival.

As the years passed by, I realized my dad did not strive for success. For whatever reason, he relied on my mother and his children to support the family. Growing older did not make him any wiser. Although Daddy dreamed big, every time he had a little money, he would blow it. During those bleak times, there was a small measure of comfort when he admitted he wished that there were more that he could do for us.

On a positive note, the quality I most appreciated in my father was honesty. Sometimes the answer he gave was not the one I wanted, but he never lied. Daddy had no respect for a liar or a thief, and he wasn't either one.

In 1968, my parents finally agreed to disagree and divorced after thirty-plus years of marriage. Within a few months, finally free of their love-hate union, they were both miserable. Apparently, they couldn't live together yet couldn't live apart. I offered to take them to be remarried, and they accepted.

The rest of the family wanted no part of my parents' plans. I couldn't blame them. When we were growing up, our parents' turbulent relationship drove us crazy. As a child, I used to pray that they would divorce. My dad could be pretty ornery to my mother, and during their decades together, he abused her both physically and verbally.

I need not have worried that Daddy would have the upper hand. Mama was about as tough as he was. On one occasion, she clobbered him with a big, heavy chair, and the stars flew. So strong was the impact, that I drove him to the hospital for stitches. When he came home, they made love. Their antics never failed to amaze any of us.

Although I wasn't in favor of my parents getting back together, it was what my mother wanted. She loved him in spite of his flaws. Above all, I wanted Mama to be happy.

I called around and found a judge in Galveston who would perform the ceremony. My brother and sisters had no desire to attend, so I drove Mama and Daddy to Galveston from LaPorte. Afterward, we toasted the occasion with a bottle of wine, and on the way home, we stopped by the trailer park in LaPorte to visit Patsy and Bobbie and their families. By then, everybody seemed pleased that Mama and Daddy had once again tied the knot.

Eventually the time came for me to head back to Pasadena. I knew that Cynthia and my children would be waiting. Typical of early fall evenings in southeast Texas, the fog had rolled in close to the ground, and the road ahead looked as creepy as a Halloween tale. As I left the trailer park, I opted to save a little time by using a shortcut through Bayshore.

I was especially cautious because of the poor visibility, and I wasn't going very fast. Suddenly a barricade appeared. Instinctively, I braked and sharply veered to the right to avoid hitting the wooden sign. I felt a jolt from underneath the car as the wheels careened off the road. Seconds later, my '63 Ford sedan was airborne, flipping before finally coming to rest in a shallow ditch. I struggled to free myself from the wreckage. The car was totaled, but at least I wasn't hurt. Crawling out, I could see a security guard from a nearby refinery running across the road to help.

"Hey, mister, are you hurt?" he asked.

"I don't think so," I said. "Can't say the same for my car. Where did that sign come from?"

"Come on back to the guard shack, and you can call someone for a tow," he suggested.

I willingly followed him and phoned Bobbie, who met us at the accident scene and drove me to Pasadena. Still shaken, I counted my lucky stars.

Later that night, two LaPorte policemen appeared at our door to announce that I was under arrest because I had damaged state property. I was shocked at their accusation.

"You hit the barricade and tore it up," they claimed. "You destroyed state property. You'll have to come with us."

At the police station in LaPorte, I was placed in a dark room with a light over my head. They grilled me like a real criminal.

"You owe us money," the duo took turns repeating.

"I didn't touch anything," I said over and over. "I took to the ditch to avoid hitting the barricade. Somebody else must have hit it. I can understand how it happened: there was fog on the ground."

I could see that this pair wasn't budging. In fact, I think they enjoyed playing both judge and jury, while brandishing their big flashlights. That night, though, they met their match. I, too, could be stubborn.

"Let me tell you something: I'm not paying for something I didn't do," I said. "You can take that to the bank. What if I had been killed due to your inefficiency? I should be suing you! You set me up with a court date, and I'll be back with my attorney."

They could see that my mind wasn't going to change. By the next morning, a court date was set. When my attorney accompanied me to the hearing several weeks later, the district attorney seemed eager to settle.

"We're willing to let bygones be bygones here," he said. "You're free to go."

The beginning of my parents' new life together was also an eventful ordeal for me.

28.

By 1970, I had made quite a name for myself in the industry, but not everyone was thrilled with my success. That year I was promoted to senior vice president of Lehn & Fink, and fellow employees did everything they could to disrupt my work. There were some bad feelings, but there was no denying that my success caused others to be better salesmen.

In the six years that followed, many manufacturers opted for representation by brokers. Lehn & Fink followed suit, and became associated with the Dan Lawrence Company, a brokerage firm of about twenty-five employees. I agreed to become part of this local firm. The owner, a sharp dresser with good looks to match, was a terrific salesman, and I respected his opinion. At his company, my sales figures continued to climb. Dan and I always spoke frankly to each other, including one morning when he came into my office with an observation.

"You're one of the best I've ever seen," he said. "We've all got faults, and I'm going to tell you what yours are."

"Okay," I said, bracing myself. "Tell me. I can take it."

"The job's not done until the paperwork is done, and you're lousy at completing it," he said.

"Then hire me a secretary to do the paperwork," I said. "You can't afford to pay me what you're paying me to do paperwork."

Within days, I had a personal secretary in an office set apart from the main office.

Dan himself was not without fault. More than once his champagne taste and beer budget got him into trouble. In addition, he had a serious drinking problem. When he was sober, he was good to me and good to work with. When he was drunk, he jeopardized our future. In time, I could stand it no more.

"Look, it's your company, but it would be in our best interest if you didn't drink up here," I said. "You'll run off more customers than I can bring in."

Dan and I disagreed on many things, but I knew that he listened to me. Eventually, he complied, and began to trust me with the reins. Not having him there for guidance was difficult at first, but his absence gave me a chance to gain some valuable experience running the business.

While climbing the corporate ladder, I willingly became a workaholic and jumped on any outside opportunity to make an extra dollar. During the next few years, I bought three rental houses and a barber shop in Spring Branch. From there, I started a janitorial service that cleaned floors for area supermarkets. Of all the ventures I entered, my favorite was a convenience store. From the time I worked at Griffin Grocery, I had always wanted to own a store and was thrilled to purchase a rundown market not far from home. In time, Cynthia and I spruced up its appearance and established a clientele of regular customers. To make the property even more profitable, I also bought and sold pre-owned cars in its parking lot.

On the home front, Cynthia stayed busy raising our four children. By now, Jack, Robert, and Lisa were active in high school activities and the challenges they presented. Jack enjoyed music and excelled as a trombone player in band, while Robert, who favored athletics, became a fine baseball player. Lisa thrived on challenges and worked hard to make top grades. Little Amy reveled in elementary school.

When the kids were in class during the day, Cynthia worked in the convenience store and increased our investment by adding homemade deli sandwiches to the mix. The demand for fresh sandwiches was so great that Cynthia hired additional help to assemble three to four hundred a day. By now, Robert was old enough to join her once school dismissed in the afternoons.

Robert's participation in the store typified his life. From the very beginning of his life, he had been a little man. He was an early walker with a sense of independence that only grew with age. A charmer, Robert was always laughing and joking, but he was also aggressive, no matter what activity he pursued. He made time for everybody—even the elderly and young kids in our neighborhood—and drove the teachers crazy with trivia questions. Robert was equally popular with his classmates.

Like I had in my own days at Griffin Grocery, Robert learned early how to please the customers. The hours between 2 and 5 are usually the slowest part of the day in that type of business, but they became our busiest. Robert memorized what type of beer each customer liked and would have their drinks already bagged when they arrived.

Robert stopped by the store to pick up his paycheck on Friday, May 19, 1979. It was a warm, clear afternoon, and he and his buddies were heading to Somerville, a farming community northwest of Houston, to spend the weekend. Afterward, he stopped by the house to tell Cynthia good-bye and pick up his fishing gear. Neither of us suspected that

Robert would not arrive safely; he was a good driver, and we trusted him.

Cynthia and I were deep in slumber when our phone rang around midnight. My wife sat straight up in bed, but I was the one who picked up the receiver. The shaky voice on the other end belonged to Shawn Sullivan, a good friend of Robert's.

"Mr. Caldwell," he said, gasping, "there's been a terrible accident."

My heart stopped. "Is Robert okay?" I cried, struggling to gather my wits.

"Well, he's … he's …"

A series of sobs and shuffles followed. I could tell that Shawn had broken down. Finally a nurse from the hospital in Hempstead grabbed the phone to complete the sentence.

"I'm sorry, Mr. Caldwell, but your son has been killed," she said.

Cynthia sensed what had happened without being told. We later learned that Robert and his friends had left Houston later than planned. When they approached Prairie View, Robert swerved to avoid unmarked construction and ran off the shoulder of the road. He steered to veer back into traffic, but he overadjusted and landed directly in the path of a truck towing a racecar. Robert's passenger, as well as the truck's driver and his son, were also killed instantly.

Burying my son was the hardest thing that I've ever had to do. Losing Billy Ray had been my first experience with death, and I now fully understood the grief that my parents must have felt. A part of Cynthia and me died with Robert that night. As a Christian, you don't question those situations because there is no answer. I know my son would want me to make each day meaningful in some way, and that's what I have always attempted to do.

29.

After Robert died, Cynthia asked me to stay close to home. She didn't speak about Robert very often, but I could sense her deep sadness. At her request, I sold the store. There were just too many memories there for her to bear returning to work.

In time, the grief that I felt from losing our son was compounded by restlessness. Too much idle time led to boredom. Deep down, I knew I needed a challenge, something more to occupy my mind. As the days passed, I realized that nothing would bring Robert back. It became more difficult to work for Dan, yet the fact remained that my wife and children needed me, and I still needed to make more money.

One day, after visiting Robert's grave, I came home and voiced my idea. "Hey, I've had a lot of time to think about it, and I'm going to start my own brokerage business," I told Cynthia. "If I'm not working, I feel like I'm wasting my time."

In her typical style, my wife responded positively. "Well, if that's what you want to do, I'll be there for you," she said. I felt fortunate to hear the blessing that I treasured the most.

When Dan sold his company to a Dallas firm the following year, the timing seemed right for me to leave. After all those years of working to make a profit for someone else, I was ready to be my own boss. There were no hard feelings, and my fellow employees wished me well. As it turned out, resigning was the easy part.

I always knew that anything could be accomplished if I just put my mind to it, and that Cynthia would be there to support me. At least I had that going for me. Because I knew so many people in the business, I thought that there would be no problem recruiting clients to represent. I surmised that this new venture would be a piece of cake. In reality, I was about to face one of the biggest dilemmas of my life.

To say the start-up process proved more difficult than expected is an understatement. My marketing plan was simple. I began by sending letters to all of my contacts in the trade. Believing that the phone would ring off the hook, I signed the lease on a small office in north Houston. To my dismay, the weeks passed slowly, and no one called to sign up. Within a few months, I lost more than two hundred thousand dollars and felt as broke as a convict.

I was forced to face the music when my banker called me into his office. "Do you think this brokerage business is ever going to amount to anything?" he asked.

His question only fueled my determination. "Well, I'm not ready to throw in the towel just yet," I answered.

"You know we'll do what we can for you," he replied in a less-than-enthusiastic tone. He forced a smile and walked away.

On the drive home, I thought about everything it took to make the business work. To raise operating capital, I sold my other businesses. Even with an office, I couldn't afford a secretary. Fortunately, Trudy, the receptionist who worked for the company next door, was kind enough to help. In fact, I had my phone set up so that it would ring in her office.

Cynthia, who had never worked in an office, found an administrative job with good pay to help make ends meet. *What else does it take?* I thought, recalling the rough hurdles in my life. Somehow, I felt certain that this road, although bumpier than ever, was worth taking.

That night after we climbed into bed, Cynthia also voiced her concern. "Jackie, do you think the business is going to make money?"

"Funny you should ask," I said. "That's the same question I heard at the bank this afternoon."

"Well, I don't care if we lose everything," she said, looking up at me with those big green eyes. "I'm behind you all the way."

My wife's vote of confidence meant the world to me. I'll never know if it was because of her encouragement, but after months of struggling to keep Caldwell Brokerage afloat, things finally started to turn around.

Finally I landed an interview with Luden's—a potentially large client—but I didn't want to take any chances. After all, walking into a bare office with no employees would make their management wonder if I were successful enough to broker their products. A strong, prosperous image was essential.

"Hey, can you come over here during your lunch hour and help me?" I asked Cynthia. Eager to oblige, my wife agreed to play the role of my secretary.

I also recruited Trudy to call during the interview process and pretend to place a big order. To my delight, the strategy worked, and I landed the Luden's account.

The following week, the three of us repeated this little scenario with Hills Brothers Coffee, another sizeable account. Once again, our one-act play worked like a charm. Hills Brothers signed with Caldwell Brokerage. As a salesman, I certainly wasn't going to make any sales by sitting in my office all day. I needed to be out among the prospects, talking to everyone, whether or not they were in the market for the products I sold. Once people know what you need, I'm convinced they'll help you out. The same concept held true when I started Caldwell Brokerage.

One of the clients I set my sights on was the Texas Department of Corrections. Long before 1980, my family and I regularly attended the Texas Prison Rodeo in Huntsville, about fifty miles north of Houston. Staged on the grounds of the state's oldest prison institution, the annual event featured convicts in rodeo acts, ranging from bull riding and calf roping to cowboy clowns. The musical entertainment showcased both nationally known and upcoming performers. Small wonder the popular outdoor show garnered a regular spot on my fall calendar. The future of Caldwell Brokerage was about to change course.

As fate would have it, mentioning the rodeo advanced my business dealings with the department's purchasing agent. Always dressed in a dark suit, Wayne Boatwright reminded me of a hanging judge. My perception was reinforced while waiting for an appointment outside his office one afternoon. I could overhear him chastising an inmate for using profanity.

"If I ever hear you say another four-letter word, I'll have your trial and jury right here," Wayne bellowed, slamming his hand on the desk. Taken aback, I figured he had to be tough. Projecting a mean, no-nonsense image was crucial in that environment. In reality, he proved to be a kind and considerate soul.

To my relief, our meeting was pleasant. "I just love this rodeo y'all have," I said, trying to sell myself as well as my business.

"If you want to come this year, I'll show you where to ask for tickets," he said. "There's one small area that's in the shade."

Anyone who attended the rodeo, staged in early fall, knew about the sweltering heat and humidity. I quickly accepted Wayne's thoughtful offer, not simply to enjoy a cool spot to watch the competitions, but because he had tickets in the same section. We could talk, visit, and perhaps do a little business. Indeed we did.

Wayne and I had a standing appointment at 6 in the morning every two weeks. In time, we developed a solid business relationship. Our friendship grew as well. Through trial and error, I learned about every facet of feeding the prison population. I was interested to learn that only about 5 percent of inmates had any money of their own. The state furnished three meals a day, and the inmates who were considered indigent received a daily allowance to purchase items such as toiletry goods, underwear, and snacks. My business included snacks, so I set out to offer a wide variety, not just cookies and crackers—which inmates refer to as "hits"—but other goodies such as sardines, peanut butter, and candy.

I also learned that each cell contained a hot pot. From my Arkansas State dorm days, I knew firsthand that selections from soup to spaghetti could be successfully cooked in this simple appliance. Offering a broader range of products became my mission.

30.

Initially, one factor that I didn't consider is that issues other than hunger might impact the purchasing habits of those who were incarcerated. This realization came to light through a simple candy bar made by Hollywood Brands. The company made Zero, Payday, and Butternut bars, and all three were big sellers in Texas. I believed that the same would hold true with customers in the Texas prisons.

When I introduced Hollywood's products to Wayne, he immediately placed an order for fifty cases of Payday and Butternut. To my surprise, he refused to order Zero. Certainly, Zero, with its caramel, peanut, and almond nougat, wrapped in white fudge, tasted delicious. There was no question that it was a first-class product. I was confused.

"Why don't you want any Zero bars?" I asked.

"Most of our prisoners are black, and they won't eat anything white," Wayne explained. I couldn't believe my ears.

"Sure, they will," I answered. "Everybody likes Zero."

"Not these guys," he said.

"Let's try and see," I persisted.

"I'll tell you what," he said. "I'll buy twenty-five cases. If they don't buy them, you're going to eat them." The proposition sounded fair to me. It turned out that Wayne knew the inmates better than I did. To my amazement, his prediction was right on track. After several weeks, I reluctantly bought back twenty-five cases of Zeros.

Nothing surprised me. Another interesting episode concerned vanilla wafers, manufactured by the Jackson Cookie Company. Although I personally was not a fan of the dry cookie, I liked the manufacturer, whose headquarters were located not far from Crawfordsville, in Little Rock. I tried my best to put a positive spin on the vanilla wafers when another purchasing agent, Gary Brizendine, sampled one. He wasn't one to mince words.

"Jackie, I hate to tell you, but these cookies taste like crap," he said bluntly. Although he had a quick wit and liked to jerk my chain, I knew that Gary wasn't kidding.

"But they don't get soggy when you make banana pudding," I said.

"Well, we don't make banana pudding," he replied, standing to stretch his tall frame. "Our guys eat them straight from the bag."

About that time, W. J. Estelle, the director of TDC, entered the office and glanced at the opened bag of vanilla wafers on the corner of the desk.

"Do you mind if I try one of these?" he asked, unaware of our previous discussion. Before Gary could reply, Mr. Estelle grabbed a wafer and took a big bite. To my astonishment, he smiled. "Are we stocking these?"

"No, they aren't very good," Gary answered.

"Well, I think these are the best cookies we've ever had," he said. "We need to buy some."

That was the only business dealing I ever had with Mr. Estelle. That afternoon, Gary placed a large order, and the next day, I sent Mr. Estelle his own case.

While things were looking up for Caldwell Brokerage, my mother's health was failing. Mama had battled diabetes for almost twenty years. The disease reared its ugly head once again in 1980, when she cut her toe and developed gangrene. By the time I heard about it, Bobbie had already taken her to the hospital, where a decision had been made to amputate Mama's foot. She was terrified.

"Before we start sharpening the knife, I want to get a second opinion," I alerted the doctors. My sisters and brother were not pleased that I wasn't going along with the idea. I think they had Mama's best interests in mind, but I could tell that they resented my involvement. That very day, I checked her out of the hospital and called a specialist.

After examining the infected foot, the neurosurgeon leveled with me. "Jackie, your mother has a serious problem," he said, before presenting the good news. "The worst scenario is that we'll have to remove that big toe."

Strangely, Mama's toe got well. Her physician dubbed the unlikely occurrence a divine intervention, pointing out that there was no medical reason why it should have healed. However, her problems were far from over.

"Your mother has got to quit smoking," her specialist cautioned on a follow-up visit. "She's also got to wear shoes when she goes outside. This is serious. She has no circulation, and she can't afford to cut herself."

Mama was hardheaded. Even with such a stern warning, her stubborn streak prevailed. She continued to smoke and eventually cut her foot when not wearing shoes. Before my mother's long and painful ordeal was over, doctors had no choice but to amputate her entire left leg.

It had been a decade since my parents remarried. For years, my father's problems had been compounded by jealousy, and he went so far as to resent the time that Mama spent with me.

No longer mobile, Mama required twenty-four-hour care. She detested asking for help, but to his credit, Daddy was attentive to her needs. I knew her spirits needed a boost, and I took the opportunity to spoil her whenever I had the chance. In early October of 1981, I stopped by my parents' trailer before a hunting trip.

"Mama, would you like me to bring you a couple of young squirrels?" I asked. During our Arkansas days, the furry rodents comprised one of her favorite dishes.

"Oh, yes, Jackie," she said. Her eyes lit up. "I'd really like that!"

After shooting a couple of squirrels the next day, I called to let Mama know my travel plans.

"I'm not going to make it by there today, but I'll be by tomorrow," I said.

"That's fine," she answered. "I'll see you then." Those were the last words my mother ever spoke to me. That night, she passed away from a blood clot, most likely a nasty by-product of the amputation.

Mama had always set the pace, never asking anyone to do more than she did. For her children, she provided enough love to go around, even if money was in short supply. My father, who had taken her for granted too often, keenly felt her absence. Daddy often said that he could still hear Mama hollering for him even after she was gone. Sadly, he began to drink even more. His death would come eight years later from a major stroke brought on by alcoholism.

There was some level of consolation that my parents, once sharecroppers, lived to see all of their surviving children achieve success. By that time, each of us was married with children of our own. We were all leading productive lives: Jimmy was an operator at a chemical plant, Bobbie worked in food management for the LaPorte Independent School District, Patsy was a Presbyterian minister, and Carolyn managed a coffee shop at Johnson Space Center, where NASA is located. I, of course, was just a country boy from Crawfordsville, still trying to make a small living for my family.

31.

I started Caldwell Brokerage as a retail broker, so my transactions occurred with grocery stores. Because this system required quite a bit of manpower, it proved very costly. It seemed that there were never enough people to do the job, and I found myself stretched thin.

When oil patch operations went belly up in the early 1980s, the retail business became even more difficult. Consumers were closely watching their money and were not buying as many products at the grocery store.

In order to streamline their operations, many grocery stores directed sales calls to corporate offices. For instance, if I wanted to call on Kroger, its office was in Cincinnati, Ohio. Safeway Corporation was headquartered in Pleasanton, California. Even the Texas-based H-E-B food retailer referred its calls to San Antonio. For numerous financial as well as practical reasons, I decided to concentrate on the vending business and let the retail segment go by the wayside. The time seemed right for a transition.

The first vending line that Caldwell Brokerage represented was Southern Fruit (now known as Florida Natural), an Orlando-based company that manufactured Bluebird juices. As if by clockwork, Southern Fruit's collection of beverages filled a void and grew to be a big player with my company. Encouraged by its success, I looked for more companies to come on board. Other accounts, such as Lance Foods and Bumblebee Seafood, soon followed suit.

One day I received a call from a gentleman in a familiar area. At that time, Arkansas had only one area code, so I was excited to see 501 on the message. The caller was Fred Gordon, a sales manager with Castleberry Foods, and he was coming to Texas to interview food brokers. As it turned out, Fred lived near Horseshoe Lake in Hughes, Arkansas. Through our conversation, I learned that he was an avid fisherman. Coincidentally, I had fished Horseshoe Lake many times and knew its best fishing spots like the back of my hand.

"I'm going to make you a deal that you can't turn down," I said. "Let me be your broker, and I'll show you where all the honey holes are in that lake you're living on."

Fred took my advice and appointed Caldwell Brokerage to represent Castleberry Foods. It was a smart move for both of us. Since that time, Caldwell Brokerage has been recognized several times by Castleberry Foods as the No. 1 broker in the country.

In the economic slump of the eighties, I adjusted our sales strategy to fit the economy. I knew that companies would continue to give us a quota, and meeting these expectations would likely impact our bottom line in a big way. I saw the handwriting on the wall and contacted the companies we represented to ask them to adjust our quota downward. All were very considerate in working out a new figure. Even though Caldwell Brokerage did less business during this time, the company made it through that year without losing any lines. Other companies neglected to plan for the inevitable and were not so fortunate.

Our family's budget was stretched tighter than ever. To bring in extra money, I took a weekend job butchering meat in a grocery store. My daughter, Lisa, then a college freshman, wrote to us and offered to drop out of school to save money. I insisted that she stay put and earn her degree. Somehow we managed to get by.

"Sweetie, we'll just have to add more water to the gravy," I told Cynthia. We both laughed. The business rocked along and eventually started to grow. Again, the paperwork—a fact of life in any brokerage endeavor—swallowed my productivity. I approached my wife with yet another brilliant idea.

"I know you like your job, and I would never ask you to do this, but I need a secretary," I said. "I have orders to fill, payroll and invoices to take care of, and I don't have the time. I'll let you make the call. If you want to continue working, you'll be working to pay the secretary."

"Well, I'm not working to pay someone else," she said.

Without a single complaint, Cynthia resigned from a job she loved and joined Caldwell Brokerage. She hit the ground running and took over the checkbook. Shortly thereafter, our company moved into a nice office complex in west Houston, and expanded to two rooms. As in our homes, Cynthia's natural flair for decorating took our offices to the next level. People joked with me about sleeping with my secretary. It was true.

During those next few years, the vending business fluctuated. Some of the bigger fish ate the smaller fish, rendering the business an even greater challenge. If there are one hundred players out there selling a manufacturer's products, and that number dwindles to fifty—some who are not carrying those products—times can always become difficult once again. One of the upsides of being a small business is that it's easier to make a change than it is with a large company. I learned that when business changes, you have to be flexible enough to change with it. Complacency always gives the competition an edge.

Meanwhile, I developed a master plan to increase Caldwell Brokerage's business with prisons. First, I wanted TDC to let me sell to other systems nationwide. After obtaining permission, I met with Roy Bryant, Castleberry Foods' operations manager, and talked about the ramifications of such a scheme. His company and others jumped on board, and within weeks, Caldwell Brokerage's marketing arm stretched to encompass Louisiana and Oklahoma prisons. Now we were covering three states with twenty-five manufacturers. From there, the business grew by leaps and bounds to include prison systems in other states from coast to coast.

I have crisscrossed the United States and seen the inside and outside of prisons. Unfortunately, our incarcerated population is growing too fast. When I first called on TDC as a salesman with Lehn & Fink in 1962, the system housed about five thousand inmates. As of 2008, that figure approached two hundred thousand. In sheer numbers of prison residents, only California rivals Texas.

I was, and continue to be, open to innovation and improvement. One example is the foil pouch, a packaging technique born of necessity. I had the idea because Chilean canned mackerel, a favorite of inmates, was only available in a fifteen-ounce can. When concealed in a sock, the metal lid could be used as a weapon. Once I convinced the San Pedro Mackerel Company to invest in the expensive equipment to vacuum pack their product, the rest was history. Thanks to the foil pouch, a broader line of products, such as tamales, is now available to prison occupants. Other companies soon adopted the pouch, which continues to receive rave reviews among consumers.

Caldwell Brokerage has weathered a lot of storms. I remain enormously proud of our associations and the fact that although we have resigned some accounts, our services have never been terminated.

Unlike the previous decade, which was peppered with heartache, struggle, and uncertainty, the 1990s blessed us with good fortune. Jack, Lisa, and Amy were now adults, and Cynthia and I relished our new roles as both in-laws and grandparents of eight.

Our business continued to expand. Lisa, who joined the company after graduating from college in 1987, worked side by side with me to facilitate that growth. In 1998, we hired sales representative Richard Cameron, and several years later, Randy Welch came on board as our information technology administrator. By the turn of the century, the company's revenue had reached one million dollars.

32.

The success of Caldwell Brokerage allowed me to indulge my sweetheart, who had stood by my side when times were rough. We traveled throughout the United States and even visited Europe and the Orient, soaking in the sights I had learned about years earlier in Coach Watson's history class. Every December, our holiday season began in New York City, where we treated ourselves to Broadway shows and Christmas shopping. In summer, Jackson Hole, Wyoming, where we had previously vacationed as a family, became our favorite getaway as a couple. There, I taught Cynthia to fly fish, and with beginner's luck, she caught more fish than I did.

My wife and I were living the American dream, but we both agreed that it was time to start giving back. We always believed that if we had more money than what we needed, it should be shared. In my case, that list included Miss Catherine and Miss Jane. They had been my special angels in tough times, and I took great pleasure in spoiling them. I never let a birthday, Easter, Christmas, or any other major holiday go by without making sure that they had fresh flowers. If possible, I traveled to Arkansas and treated them to dinner. Each of these fine Southern ladies came to love Cynthia as the daughter they never had.

There was other unfinished business in Arkansas. All these years, Billy Ray's burial site had gone unmarked. I returned to Parkin in 1995 to do something about it.

"I'd like to put a marker on my brother's grave," I told the caregiver, who eyed me suspiciously when I appeared at her office. Once I explained the circumstances, she nodded and offered to drive me to the cemetery.

To my disappointment, the property, which had opened for business in the 1880s, was in terrible condition. More than forty years had passed since the day Billy Ray was buried, and now waist-high weeds concealed many of the gravesites. Since I was just a kid back then, I wasn't sure I could remember his exact location. It wasn't that Parkin Cemetery lacked business; Parkin was just a poor town without any funds for proper maintenance.

The caretaker examined a wrinkled chart. "You say your brother was Billy Ray Caldwell?" she asked. "You're standing just a few feet from him."

I stared lovingly at the unkempt ground and forced myself to recall that icy winter day when I bid good-bye to my little brother. So much had happened in the last four decades, but the memory of our bond had never faded.

In addition to installing a granite marker for Billy Ray, I refurbished the cemetery by clearing and landscaping the grounds, then properly marking the entrance with a wrought-iron fence and brick columns. I knew it was time for the citizens of Parkin to have a dignified resting place. Since then, the property has been maintained through donations as well as the labor of the local garden club. Now people feel good about going to visit their deceased relatives in that cemetery.

Cynthia and I usually reserved our annual getaway to Jackson Hole for July and August, when the searing heat and humidity of the Texas Gulf Coast were at their peak.

"I hate Houston this time of year," my wife would complain when her allergies flared up. "I wish we could go to Wyoming and stay the whole summer."

In mid-2003, I noticed that Cynthia was coughing more than usual. Leaving for vacation a bit earlier seemed a small price to pay for her comfort.

By June, the clear skies and fresh air of Wyoming beckoned. Instead of flying as we had in the past, Cynthia asked if we could drive and see the scenery along the way. I thought her request a bit unusual, but I agreed that it would be fun. That year, my wife and the weather could not have been more beautiful. During those two weeks, we fished and relaxed day after day. Simply enjoying each other's company made this vacation particularly memorable, although somehow I knew, as I think Cynthia did, that she was very sick. There are just certain things you know after being married for so long.

When we returned to Houston, Cynthia's coughing grew worse. At first we blamed it on the weather—at least that's what we hoped. However, in the months that followed, the constant coughing turned to choking. More than once, she was unable to catch her breath. Cynthia put on a happy face, but it was obvious that her energy and patience were wearing thin. Deep down, we both knew that it was time for answers. I hoped and prayed for a quick solution to ease her pain and make her well once again. Unfortunately, the diagnosis did not come easily.

The day our longtime family physician called me at work, I knew that Cynthia's test results were serious. My wife's irregular blood pressure provided yet another clue.

"I need you to bring Cynthia to my office," Dr. Madeline Domask said. The tone of her voice was uncharacteristically somber.

"I guess it's bad news?" I said, struggling with a lump in my throat.

"Well, it's treatable," she said softly. No one needed to tell me that treatable did not mean curable.

When Dr. Domask shared the findings—cancer, although she was not sure of what type—Cynthia was remarkably calm. "I've had a good life, but I would love to see my grandkids grow up," she said with determination. "I'm not going to give up yet."

I tried to be strong, although the shock of the diagnosis floored me. I wanted to wake up from this nightmare, to know that Cynthia and I would be together in our golden years. I knew she had given me so many more memories than most people have in a lifetime, but I just wasn't ready to say good-bye.

I had already participated in more funerals in 2004 than I cared to attend. That year Miss Catherine succumbed to cancer at the age of eighty-four, and I was a pallbearer. Years earlier, I had paid her back the money she gave me for college.

"Keep it," she had insisted. "No way," I said. "I know you don't need it, but perhaps it can help someone else." Financially, my debt was settled, yet I could never repay the kind encouragement she offered in my formative years.

Miss Catherine never asked for anything, but the favor she requested at our last meeting broke my heart. "I carried you, now you're going to carry me," she said. Her back may have been hurting from cancer, but her mind was sharp until the end.

Three months later, Miss Jane died. I didn't know if I could bear another loss, especially that of my soul mate.

More tests, more doctors, more hopes dashed in the weeks to come. Finally, the verdict—plasmacytoma, a rare type of blood cancer—was delivered by Cynthia's oncologist, who didn't mince words.

"It's bad," he admitted. "She may live six months to a year. There hasn't been much research done on this type of cancer."

We studied the black and white transparency and listened intently as he pointed to the culprits. A tumor snaking around Cynthia's esophagus and another below her left breast were the cause of her coughing.

Hoping against hope, I sought the opinions of world-renowned experts, but their conclusions were always the same. There was no research, no protocol for the type of cancer she had.

33.

To take Cynthia's mind off of her illness, I found a new site for Caldwell Brokerage in northwest Houston. The extra space was perfect for our needs, but the land, building, and warehouse would require some work.

"I'll only buy it if you promise to decorate it inside and out," I told Cynthia, knowing that she couldn't resist the challenge. Working hand in hand with a builder, our new headquarters were finished within six weeks.

Cynthia's coughing became more frequent. Refusing to accept defeat, we directed specialists to fight the enemy the best way they knew how. Strong radiation burned her lungs, and within six months, she lapsed into a coma. I helplessly watched as her condition deteriorated.

Unable to breathe on her own, Cynthia was placed on a ventilator. Certain she would never want such treatment, I ordered doctors to remove her from the machine. They agreed, but in a last-ditch effort, they performed a tracheotomy to deliver air to her lungs.

"Did somebody die?" was the first question Cynthia asked when she woke up from the coma.

"No, sweetie, nobody died," I said.

"Are you sure?" she whispered.

Cynthia recovered from the episode with her mind intact; however, it was as if her body had suffered a stroke. She became an invalid and needed therapy. Much like a stroke victim, Cynthia had to learn to walk and feed herself all over again. She did so with flying colors.

During her last two years, we were together twenty-four hours a day, seven days a week. I tried my best to make Cynthia comfortable. On days when we did not go to the doctor, we didn't go anywhere. That's just the way it was.

As usual, my wife found happiness in doing for others. In December of 2005, she decorated a Christmas tree for every grandchild's bedroom. Cynthia always loved the holidays, and although no one said it, the gesture was bittersweet. We all knew that it was her last Christmas.

Eventually, Cynthia relied on oxygen to breathe. Always, her spirit was stronger than her body. To this day, I don't know how she mustered the energy to travel to Crawfordsville for my class reunion the following May. Perhaps she knew that I would never go without her. Our daughters offered to join us. Imagine my shock, when after dinner, my wife announced it was time to bugaloo.

"Hon, you'll be in the hospital before the night is out," I cautioned.

"I don't care," she quipped, leaning on Lisa and Amy for support.

Scarcely three weeks after we returned home, Cynthia struggled to sleep. I spent most of the night rocking her like a little baby. In the early hours of June 11, 2006, I carried her back to our bedroom.

"Don't leave," she said as I gently placed her on top of the sheets. "Lay down next to me."

I climbed in bed and held her, hoping she could now breathe easier. At long last, rest seemed inevitable. Cynthia's head slipped off the pillow, and I climbed out of bed to adjust it.

"What are you doing?" she asked, drowsily.

"I'm just straightening your pillow," I answered.

I gazed at Cynthia, still so beautiful in the darkness. It was then that I noticed that her chest no longer moved up and down. I could tell that her lungs had collapsed and were no longer gasping for air. Cynthia's death, unlike the last two years of her life, was very peaceful.

34.

With Cynthia gone, I've had time to really think about my life. From the time I was twelve years old, which I believe to be the age of reason, I prayed to the good Lord to point me in the right direction. Somehow I knew I had to make the right choices.

For years, I watched my mother and father chop cotton from sun up to sundown—a job that netted only three dollars a day—in the summer heat. After twelve-hour days in the fields, other tasks waited at home. Milking cows, slopping the hogs, tilling the garden, and pumping water never seemed to end. As kids, we were expected to help. It was a hard life, and together, we struggled to survive. There's no doubt in my mind that today I would rather have a rattlesnake following me than a cotton sack.

In everything I did, choosing the path between right and wrong was always in the back of my mind. When faced with a decision, it always came down to staying on the right road. Even so, the road was not always smooth and even. More often than not, it took a twist. Sometimes it was bumpy, and other times it was muddy. Once in a while, it flooded.

By the time I was a teenager, some of my friends were mischievous, and I admit to getting off the road a few times. Yet, I consider myself lucky in a lot of ways. I sometimes did things that I knew were morally wrong and of which I wasn't very proud. Fortunately, I always realized the error of my ways and where that road was going to lead. I thank God for people who loved and cared for me after I left home. If I got off on the wrong road, some friends, like Miss Catherine, who watched me like a hawk, were instrumental in bringing me back.

Ultimately, my decision to stay on the right path may have cost me a friend or two, but now I know that the people I lost were not the friends for me. Today I probably give more advice than what I took in my younger years. I've always tried to communicate with my children and grandchildren and will always be here for them. Of course, I don't expect any more of them than I did of myself.

If you live, you learn. So many times in life, even as an adult, I came to a fork in the road and knew that it was time to evaluate myself. What I learned is that the devil works hard all the time, too. Never have I found myself face down on a road from which I could not pick myself up. Many times that meant charting new territory, whether in business or in love.

When a friend recently shared her old family recipe for fudge pie, I knew that it was time for Caldwell Brokerage to launch its first individually packaged dessert. It was also time to get on with my life. My personal philosophy is that with a lot of determination, a great future awaits anyone who is not afraid of hard work.

When I first started writing this book, I could not imagine ever sharing my heart with another woman. In my loneliness, my mind was just not open to such a possibility. Little did I know that on the rockiest of roads, the good Lord had a surprise. Today I believe that Mama, Miss Catherine, Miss Jane, and my beloved Cynthia interceded on my behalf.

Just as they had been my angels on earth, they never stopped looking out for me—even in the hereafter.

I recently married Gin, a sister of a childhood friend and the keeper of the fudge pie recipe. At the age of sixty-nine, I have fallen in love and feel as though my story is beginning all over again. Life is sweet.